A Cynical Guide to Job Hunting & Interviews

Strategies to Secure Jobs In the Most Trying Times

RICK LAZARUS

"If Opportunity Doesn't Knock,
Build a Door."

(Milton Berle)

Content

3. The Interview

Preface

"The magician prefers to keep his audience in the middle."

Welcome dear readers to the world of unadulterated cynicism. At the time of writing (which is November 2020), there's already a great amount of cynicism in the air, and it feels rather surreal for us to have come this far- when we look back retrospectively at the whole year, and how events quickly unfold.

All of a sudden, facemasks and lockdowns became the norm, and the moment anyone step outside the house, we could only see faceless human shapes, greeted with wary eyes and suspicion. The Covid-19 pandemic is definitely making people more paranoid and distrusting, towards one another, and every other aspects of society, because most people felt that a large part of society somehow failed them.

There's a belief that it could be controlled much earlier in the year if the authority had been more attentive and responsible. And now we have to face the consequences. As countries are preparing the next waves of the virus and the subsequent lockdowns, people are getting increasingly restless and uncertain about what the future holds, despite promises of the vaccine in the horizon, because they already feel the effect of the virus, which is far more extensive than just health and safety concerns, but rather whole economies and livelihoods.

At the current juncture, many sectors and businesses are getting destroyed one by one, often irreversibly so, and at a rapid rate. As a result, there are massive unemployment happening right now, across every nation throughout the world, and situation is likely going to get more desperate.

My third book under this series is about the search for jobs and opportunities, and for some reason it is even more appropriate now in this Covid-19 reality. I admit that it has become increasingly harder to secure job opportunities these days, due to job scarcity and increased competitions. But there's a recurring theme in the book which I want to emphasize here: **it doesn't matter when you are searching for a job,- when you're off the median, you will stand better chances of success than everyone else, whether during stabler and better times, or in trying times like this**.

To rephrase it, what I am trying to do here is to get the readers off the middle, into the outliers. If this sounds confusing to you, do not worry, as I will be talking about these concepts a great deal in the book. This just happens to be one of the many contrarian ideas I have in the book, although a rather significant one. If you've been following my other books, you'll know that I always take a contrarian view of things. But you see, being a contrarian is not good enough, it is far more important to be a contrarian who is correct. You'll find me putting a critical lens over some other contrarian ideas that are popularized by career experts, for example, like some of the guerrilla job hunting tactics.

When I write the book, I also consciously attempt not to follow the formulaic approach to make this book like any other book about job search; my intention is to write a really helpful one that work in the current context. I constantly reference concepts and cross examine their applicability from the other books and came to a stark realization that while these books are written with the best intent, they have become too anachronistic for our times, which is a polite way to say that they cannot be applied anymore.

Several ideas are simply not relevant in the current world, much less a Covidian world as we speak. Here are some examples of outdated ideas that should be discarded in the last millennium: it's important to get an MBA, you should follow your passion, the more jobs you apply the more chances of getting them, you should start networking extensively, you should consider internship/working for free to gain experience, you should get recruitment agents to help you in your job search, and the list goes on. I will prove that all these are wrong in the book.

I also thought it might be helpful to inject my thoughts and insights from my experiences in the job recruitment industry (significantly long enough, though shorter than my overall commercial career), which had given me enough exposure (and deep cynicism) to give the readers a very accurate and realistic view on what is really happening over there; if you find me alluding to something negative here, you're probably correct.

The readers will benefit from understanding that there are many deceptions going on in the business, and to be wary, cautious and wise when dealing with them, so that valuable time, resources and even reputation are not wasted or lost.

If you're feeling dejected or tense about the current situation and circumstances concerning your job search, be assured that this will not last for long, as long as you are able to know where to find, and start to look where nobody look- you will find opportunities that were not apparent before. You need not even have to wait till post-Covid, when everything seemingly revert back to more stability and normalcy (the whole post-Covid world will not remotely resemble any normalcy you used to know though), such opportunities may even present themselves in this most trying times, like now.

Good luck!

Rick Lazarus 2020 (*Sic itur ad astra*)

1. Preparation Work

I assume that most of the readers here are looking around for opportunities. Maybe some of you have just emerged into the job market, while others are looking to leave the current job, or have been jobless. Most of us have been through it before, but this year 2020 is quite different. We're probably going to find it harder to secure job opportunities for a while, because of the damages that the Covid-19 pandemic had done unto the economy, which causes many people to get laid off, and businesses to collapse.

When the world was in a more stable state, periods of unemployment are often felt like just a temporary impasse. But this time round, it makes people feel like they are stuck in a cul-de-sac, a seemingly hopeless situation where there's no breakthrough in sight. The desperation is stretched out over the indefinite gaze into the future, and as time is ticking away, a day without job means a day without income.

Most people only understand one way of getting an income, and that is through gainful employment. As a result, many are getting increasingly frustrated, anxious, then exhausted and depressed.

A brand-new day still looms near the horizon. All is not lost as long as you are healthy and willing. Take a deep breath and start looking around you. There are many people who are just like you. If anything, you found yourself a perfect excuse to blame for your lack of success in your job search, where applicable.

Blame it on Covid-19, and outsource all your negativity away onto this bloody virus and things associated with it. What do you do next? Whether you are still gainfully employed or not, it is time to embrace change, because you are right smack in the beginning of change, where the world transits from one type to the other, regardless of you changing or not. Knowing about this certainty, you will be better off prepared for the challenges ahead.

This pandemic no doubt is a serious crisis, primarily a health one, and having lasting effects on the economy. Yet, this pandemic in a way, is seen as a catalyst to usher us into a new digital age. Within this crisis lurks opportunity, only depending on where you look.

Most of the world is stuck in a certain doom and gloom, and will likely miss or remain blinded to the vast amounts of opportunities that are available in the present and the future. If you were like those people above, maybe it's time to get out from the median and get into the outlier, where the others within this significant tail who are enjoying relative successes right now.

Do you know that there are people thriving off this pandemic? They seemingly uncover a lot of opportunities within this period. Do not assume that they are people from the elite class where they have it easy; they are just like you and me, people largely from the working class. But they are doing something smarter than most people.

What they did was simply to look elsewhere from where all the rest was looking, and which is really the whole point of the book. I want my readers to get out of the median, a place where the masses huddle comfortably together during fair weather, and which can turn into a cesspool (and contribute to statistics) at a moment's notice when shit hits the fan. And head into the uncharted territories where normal folks tend to avoid or not know.

I can almost certainly guarantee that these uncharted territories are the best ways to beat the odds and get ahead, for your job searches. This is where the contrarians go, when the others are not looking, and secure themselves jobs right before everyone's eyes. In order to reach there, the contrarians need to have certain insights, knowledge and attitude to traverse this unmarked frontier.

We can begin by discussing the (hidden) reality of the current job market, or any job market, as well as the practices, psychology and even tricks they frequently employ. We will then look at novel tools, strategies and tactics which are off radar to even most of the other career coaches/authors of books or material that talk about job searches. Without further ado, let's get started.

The Most Qualified May Not Get the Job- The Psychology of Hiring

Have you ever wondered why good jobs frequently go to those who are undeserving in your eyes, while at the same time feeling dejected for either getting left out or getting sidelined by such opportunities? Well, you're not alone if you think like that, because this is actually a common phenomenon in the job market, where the best jobs simply do not go to the most qualified.

In order to get a grip on what the hell is going on, it is important to first congratulate yourselves, even if you have doubted your ability all along. And that is, all of the readers here, of reasonable intelligence, are actually more than qualified than you think you are for your dream jobs (for your industry), provided that you can secure such opportunities in the first place.

As Richard Branson, business magnate famous for founding of Virgin Group once famously said, "If somebody offers you an amazing opportunity but you are not sure you can do it, say yes – then learn how to do it later!" But you need to be able to pass through the front gate first.

The problem for most people is that they are kept outside the front gate by the gatekeepers, or may not even be aware that such a gate exists in the first place (we will talk more extensively about this part in the next chapter). If a person did not get the gatekeeper to open this portal, there's no chance to ever show what he or she is truly worth even when this job is perfectly made for the person.

Sometimes the gatekeepers make decisions, but otherwise they are just someone who control access. If they do not make decisions, there's another person the jobseeker needs to deal with later in order to secure the jobs- the potential boss to report to.

Getting to the final boss may not necessarily guarantee any chance of success either, regardless of whether you are the most qualified person for the job. He or she is certainly like you, a sentient being fully capable of subjective thoughts, bias and prejudices that humanity is susceptible to, and may commit the folly of not wanting you even if you are the most qualified.

In order to stand a better chance of securing any jobs, it is of critical importance to really understand and comprehend the psychology of hiring by the decision maker, so it will prepare you to act accordingly, which are cynical observations that go deeper than the superficiality of love and light platitudes. There's nothing about hiring that is fluffed up like the bullshit spewed forth by career consultants- like passion, education, job fit- these are all things that don't really matter. What matters most are how the hirers see and perceive the candidates, as well as how it can fit within his or her personal agenda. Let's first look at why there's even an employment market in the first place.

Jobs are created to get people to come onboard to solve problems. If there are no problems, there wouldn't be any need for jobs in the first place. Depending on the kind of problems, the skillsets of the workers play a part in contributing in the solutions. But there are also non-work-related problems that are harder to solve, which are affairs dealing with the troublesome creatures known as human beings.

Decisions made are often not based on rational thought processes, but frequently overridden by prejudices and biases. For those who are interested to know more about work and office politics, the readers might want to check out my first book, "A Cynical Guide to Office Jobs & Office Politics".

A candidate who are successful in securing jobs tend to fulfill most of the criteria below, particularly the first two ones. Here is a list of the criteria, ranked in descending order of importance, which strongly affect the chances of job offers:

1. **Agreeability**- This is ranked number one, and the most important of it all. Never mind if you're the genius champion who can potentially lead the organization to stellar heights; if you are not someone whom the hirer finds agreeable, you'll simply not get the job. Agreeability is all about how this person is likely to obey and carry out instructions, be friendly and cooperative

enough towards the boss and the co-workers to work as a member of a team, and how this person will not potentially sabotage or generate headaches for the hirer.

Nobody wants a difficult person to be around, especially a belligerent brat who is capable of insubordination, because work and life are hard enough for the boss, and every boss likes to maintain his or her authority. This is the reason why cronyism is still rampant amongst the work industries, which is unfortunate but an understandable part of hiring psychology.

2. **Potential Threat**- The attitude is one thing, but the next thing to worry about for every hirer (as in hirer who will also serve as potential boss of the candidate) is on whether this candidate will eventually become a potential threat to the authority or even job security for oneself. You see, while most hirers want to get people onboard to solve work problems, they do not want these people to do better than them or even to impress their own boss, which in return will create additional problems in a more personal sense, the most severe being having his or her position taken over by such potential usurper.

When they feel like the candidate can potentially jeopardize their career, in the near or far term eventually, they would rather not have this person around. Therefore, having the best qualifications for a job may not necessarily bade well for the candidate, but may even turn into a big red flag to those insecure hirers. And the unfortunate thing is that a large part of humanity is insecure.

3. **Value**- Value for the hirers is usually inversely proportional to the value for the candidates. While the candidates would really want a job that pays well, the hirer wants a workhorse (slave) who can productively generate the most benefits for the least amount of cost.

Here, the qualifications of the candidate finally come into play, where the education, experience and skillsets of such candidates are matched to the job descriptors. If the candidate is able to meet the greatest cost savings for the company in relation to the qualifications available, compared to the rest of the candidates, and having met criteria 1 and 2 listed previously, then this candidate will stand a high chance of getting the job.

This part of the hiring psychology is more readily applicable to the hirers who will eventually be the potential boss/supervisor of the candidates. They may or may not be the gatekeepers that are holding the job seekers back from the front gate of job opportunities.

Accessibility and Match-
The Enemy at the Gates

"Keep your enemies closer" is a fitting proverb for the Enemy at the Gates. These enemies are of course the gatekeepers we talked about previously. To the large number of unsuccessful jobseekers and applicants, they are the main culprit which cause them their chances, hence it is appropriate to label them enemies. Yet, you want to bring them close, perhaps closer than a friend, or even turn them into your friend.

Because, as I mentioned before, if the gatekeepers allow the jobseekers to even step pass the front gate, the possibility of finally succeeding in getting the job will increase exponentially, hence they are the most critical determinant of success in your job search.

Of course, there is always the problem of not even identifying and reaching the gates and the gatekeepers, but we will leave that to the next chapter. Here, we will talk about what will happen if you've already got the resume over, and they start working on it, the psychology affecting their decision to let you pass through the gate towards success.

Now, who are the Gatekeepers that we speak of? The answer: primarily the Human Resource (HR) managers or personnel who are either tasked by a decision maker (usually the final boss the prospective employee will report to) to hunt for candidates.

The Decision Makers themselves may also double off as a gatekeeper but this is usually rarer, and more common for smaller companies without a HR person. About 95% of all Gatekeepers are the HR, and they are also responsible for most of the job postings, advertisements that you find on job boards and company websites.

While they may be tasked for the purpose of collecting resumes or identifying potential candidates (especially when they have some "talent acquisition" function in their role) and arranging interviews (sometimes between themselves and the candidates at some point), they are usually not really familiar with what is going on within the specific industries or sectors for roles they are working on. They merely just follow instructions and put up the descriptors that are previously supplied by the decision-making hirers.

They are therefore, not the person who can truly measure and know the worth of the candidate. They don't know jack shit about those technical details and terminology relevant to the particular industry for the role. But they do know that those things comprise of the certain keywords that needs to be worked on. So, one way for them to find out if the candidate is a possible fit or not to the job descriptor, is entirely based on keywords matches. The more keywords are matched, the better qualified the candidate is, to their minds, and therefore a better chance of placement.

After they skimmed through some of the keywords, they will usually look at the eligibility of the candidate, in a superficial way. The two things that frequently come to mind are: employability and doubt. Employability as the name suggests, is really about whether the person can be suitable as an employee in the organization.

For example, having the right minimal education requirement, the right professional level (especially for mid to high level positions), the years of experience, and the pay package as an indication of suitability in that job range. To the simple mind of the gatekeeper, if the requirement that was tasked by the hirer matches the person, then it is a good fit. This is once again a matching exercise, and may not be done in a common-sensical way, especially in larger organizations.

The best way to illustrate the lack of common sense is that if the candidate has a much lower pay package range than what this role entails, he or she may not be considered, even if he or she is fully qualified to do the role!

Instead of helping the candidates to level up the salary accordingly, they are more likely to drop such candidates because it's too much work for the HR, and they don't care or are not conscious about the "value" criteria from perspectives of the hirers or the benefits of the organization. HR employees in larger organizations tend to not want to trouble themselves with extra work.

Doubt, as the second consideration that constitutes the eligibility criteria is something which comes off more naturally for the gatekeeper. Significant gaps between jobs, education from institutions not held in higher esteem, and more disparagingly, background and identity, often do play a part in casting doubts during the hiring process.

On the last part about background and identity, many companies these days, especially larger ones, will immediately jump at any chance to put forth claims and virtue signal to the world and the jobseekers about how inclusive they are because they need to keep up a certain politically image to stay away from trouble. But bias and prejudice will unfortunately continue to perpetuate at the individual level, where such entrenched doubt cost qualified job applicants their opportunities.

The third criteria, which is the last but not the least influencing factor of the gatekeeper is: Preference. Now, this is even more subjective and personal than the Eligibility criteria, where there's already a significant amount of influence based on bias and prejudice.

Preference may also surface at some point during the Doubt process, but sometimes it is not even based off the curriculum vitae, but rather from petty details like, the aesthetics of the layout, the grammar accuracy, the photo profile of the candidate (attractiveness), the level of civility and friendliness, or even the tone of the application email. Without even meeting the gatekeeper initially, positive cues garnered from the application will bring the gatekeeper closer to the candidate, as a proverbial friend. If the gatekeeper instinctively feels good about certain candidate, they will more proactively recommend this profile to the decision maker.

Let's recap the selection criteria from the gatekeeper, which I've mentioned, is based on the moment they chance upon a profile on the resume of the applicant. Number one is Keyword Match. Number two is Eligibility, which consists of Employability and Doubt. And number three is Preference. In order to influence this process towards a more favorable outcome, there must be efforts targeting the three factors when building the applicant's profile, which is what this chapter is going to be about.

There are other things which are beyond the profile building and preparation work, like what happens after the gatekeeper follow up with the candidates, or how the resumes can even successfully reach and get picked up by the gatekeeper; these I will mention in other chapters.

Active and Passive Means

If you've not been living under a rock, you'd have definitely heard of LinkedIn. This is the definitive platform used by professionals from around the world to establish network and to use its online services for career and businesses.

If you've not already signed up for one, you should, because this platform frequently plays a part in the career development for professionals in the 21st century. You simply need to sign up and create a professional profile for yourself and start adding people to your network, pretty much like what Facebook and other social media platforms do, but better, because it can actually help you.

Somewhere along the career, any professionals would start looking around for new opportunities to further their career or to get a job to tide over. Having a resume handy is always laid down as the fundamental groundwork for any career search. But much of the interactions have now shifted to having an online presence in this new digital age.

The LinkedIn site, while also fully capable of serving the function as a resume, though an online one, is actually playing a much bigger role in having the ability to be a passive mean of job matching, whereby opportunities can come knocking on your door than having to actively seek them out.

In the past, most job searches are more active in nature. The job seekers will be contacting companies and hirers while responding to jobs advertised on Classifieds Ads in the papers. They will send the resumes over by mail to the addresses stated, if any, or call up the number in the ads to speak to the in-charge, and then arrange for interviews with the resumes brought along, or do mail-ins.

The processes, while tedious, can actually significantly shortens the job searches, because only those who care enough about the opportunities will do the above (thus filtering out insincere applicants and lowering competitions), and the candidates will usually get the chance to speak to or meetup the hirers. After the advent of the internet, the means to job searches have taken a dramatic change. Instead of having to take the trouble to mail out the resumes, the applicants can simply attach these electronic documents and send them over emails.

When the job boards came into existence, all contacts became restricted to only the email addresses, thus the applicants found it harder to make first impressions through the telephone or in first person unless they received email replies requesting them to do so. Due to the ease of sending applications over emails, competitions increased significantly for a popular job posting. However, on a more positive note, there are also more jobs posted than ever before.

LinkedIn brought about a new paradigm in the employment market by allowing professional profiles to be up online. Since it is an open and public network of sorts, this platform can also serve as valuable resource for employers and businesses looking to network for partnerships and hiring.

Recruiters and hirers these days always consider LinkedIn as the first go-to when there are openings in the companies to work on, and they will trawl through profiles to match the competency and approach suitable candidates. The job seekers, instead of actively looking out for opportunities, will also have passive means of getting opportunities while LinkedIn profile sits there, looking attractive and waiting for potential interests. Having said all of the above, I strongly suggest every job seeker to make full use of both the active (resumes) and passive (LinkedIn) means concurrently, to maximize the potential of the job search.

While LinkedIn can double off as a resume, it is still important to have it in word or pdf document, because much of the active process still involves the sending of these resumes over email. And it is also important to note that while both the resumes and the LinkedIn profiles are critical for every job search, the two different means are frequently at a disconnect, meaning to say that there's a chance that the hirer will read or access one over the other. At some point in this chapter, I will be writing about ways to bridge the disconnect.

Since the active and passive means are equally important, the jobseeker should do everything within their capacity to optimize the two of them in preparation work prior to the searches, to aim for the achievement of maximum outcome in job search; which is what this chapter is going to be all about.

Covering the Gap

When you're out of job, sometimes the period of unemployment can stretch out for a long time which can lead to increasing difficulty in getting accepted for prospective jobs. Things are not so bad if the period is in a matter of months, but as the period gets longer (especially when it crosses the half year mark), the difficulty of securing potential job opportunities for professionals become much harder, which can turn into a worsening vicious cycle for the unemployed.

The hirers from within the industry are seldom comfortable with candidates with very long gap of unemployment without good reason, and will often cast doubts on the suitability of getting these people on board.

Doubt is a key factor for consideration within eligibility criteria, and once it arises from within the gatekeeper like the HR person who reads the resume, it is difficult to get them to acknowledge other positive qualities which the candidate might have.

At the time of writing, we are all stuck with the covid-19 pandemic. Most of the jobseekers who are laid off and without jobs have probably been jobless for more than half a year. That may even likely to stretch out longer, depending on whether there's going to be any improvement in the unforeseeable future. However, this actually also sort of level the playing field, because it creates a good excuse to justify for long periods of unemployment, as such long gaps have now become normative for many job seekers, who can then blame it on the virus and its disastrous effects. Yes, use it to your advantage if you get queried about the gaps.

But in any case, a jobseeker may still want to cover the long periods of unemployment, both in good times and in bad times. My suggestion to all jobseeker is: do not even show such gaps in your profile, from when you are between jobs, or from your last job. Rather, find ways to visibly cover the gaps.

Well, the first thing the person need to do if they get laid off, or left the last job, is to not update the current job situation in LinkedIn at all. Let the duration in the company continue to run, with your title intact on your profile, even when you're not in the company.

If someone from the company message you on LinkedIn to ask you to update properly your last day of employment to declare you're no longer gainfully employed, you can choose to ignore the message because it's your every right to put up what is on your personal LinkedIn profile. If they get real upset and confront you, you can simply say you lost the password to your account.

To make it simple, all you're doing is to leave your profile alone and not touch it. As LinkedIn is one of those main go-to sites for recruiters to find prospective candidates, any profile with a prolonged period of unemployment will not be deemed for consideration. Only after you secure another job do you then update your profile again, and send an apology to that busybody, like oops I missed your message.

For some people, when there were huge gaps in the past when they were between jobs, they would fill it up with a fictional job and company, provided that they had some good explanations for it. No one will be able to tell the difference especially if the gaps were from long time ago.

But there's actually one strategy which is safer, more legitimate, and which can greatly improve the chances of turning those long periods of unemployment into something attractive on your profile! And that is, to cover the gap with professional reasons that imply that you are continually on the path towards career development.

Most people tend to cover up this period of unemployment with education, which is one example of career development. But if you're not going to sign up for courses (education are usually expensive), you might actually want to consider something simpler but more effective. And that is to set up your own company.

Some of the readers might go like what?! Well, let me explain. While I suggest you to set up your own company as a cover, I am not asking you to really go into business, unless you want to, which in itself is not a bad idea provided that you have such ambitions. I am merely asking you to set up a professional reason, to increase your value and employability even when you are jobless. There are some requirements though. This company has to be registered, which may or may not be that simple, depending on where you're living. For most people, it's not too difficult or expensive to get one registered, and you can always start with sole proprietorship, as long as you have some proof of business registration.

The next thing is to make sure that your business, or the front of your so-called business, has something to do with your primary profession. This may sound hard, but it is not as hard as you think it is.

Let's say that you're a hardcore engineering geek in most of your career and you go ahead and register your company as an engineering firm. You'd think that you need massive capital or products and services to properly show that you're running the show, but you really don't need to invest in a single cent. You'd be perfectly accepted for claiming that you are doing the planning all along, building your business up and getting some projects here and there without having to show any proof of doing so.

If you want to make things easier, you can even suggest that your business is dealing with something intangible, like for example marketing. Your business does not even need to be operational or running, you just need to keep it there. There's a method to the madness.

You see, when you show the hirers that you're running a business, it gives them the impression that you're strongly competent and enterprising, willing to take your skillsets to the next level to challenge yourself. If it is relevant to your profession, it is counted as additional cumulative experience of your career in this field, which is useful for your profile image. You may want to put it up on your LinkedIn profile, or you may just want to leave it in the resume, it's up to you, but having such a reason in place of the yawning gap will definitely turn around a pathetic profile into a highly valued one.

Once you are able to speak to the hirer, you can always tell them that you are willing to get back into employment because you've garnered enough experience for running this enterprise, and will agree to their terms of hiring, shutting the business down if they would prefer you to do so.

Raising Visibility on LinkedIn

Traffic is the critical determinant of success or failure for every online endeavor these days, be it e-commerce, online business, digital marketing, content creation and influencers. Given the congested amounts of sites on the internet, a website or social media profile with little or no traffic is as good as non-existent, buried away in the virtual oblivion. High web traffic means more visitors, and outreach, which can easily translate to greater exposure, monetization, advertising interest and business opportunities.

We have to treat LinkedIn profiles similarly, because more traffic also means more interests and job opportunities. If your profile is insignificantly buried away in LinkedIn, there's no way any recruiters or hirers can reach you. So, in order to increase traffic to your LinkedIn profile, you have to find ways to raise the visibility through every possible means. Here, I will suggest several ways a user can tinker with LinkedIn to achieve maximal exposure:

1. **Customize your public profile URL**- If you are using the default URL that LinkedIn assigned your profile when you create it, it is usually full of numbers with no way to tell your identity. In order to boost your SEO (search engine optimization, which is a way you can be found more easily on the internet), you might want to

customize it. You can simply go over to your profile and edit the public profile & URL to have an address that looks like www.linked.com/in/yourname

2. **Syncing your Contacts**- Before you start adding people, you might want to have all your professional contacts synced and imported into LinkedIn. The benefit of doing so is that it increases your exposure to second-degree connections from your primary contacts (which means people who are connected to your own contacts are more likely to see you and vice versa, and may possibly want to connect with you). You can sync all the contacts from the different email accounts you use, as well as mobile phone address books.

3. **Growing your Network**- The network is a numbers game for raising visibility on LinkedIn. By adding more people, you will expand your network rapidly as you will also become visible to people you don't personally know or not close to, by association with second-degree connections, who are usually other professionals in your same industry.

You will probably start with adding people you know, but it doesn't hurt to also add people you don't know from similar professions. For strangers, you're more likely to get accepted connections with professionals at your same level and below when you request a connection. For professionals more senior than you, it's a hit and miss, but they can raise the value of your profile in the eyes of others like the recruiters. A general rule of thumb is to add 5 senior professionals in your similar industry a day, for about half a year. Chances are you will get at least 2/5 acceptances by the end of the period, which translates to about 300+ senior profiles in your network.

4. **Make Profile Public-** Your profile can only be searched on LinkedIn if it is public.

5. **Enable Open to Work-** You can let recruiters and your network know that you're open to opportunities on your LinkedIn profile. There is a button on the right section of the profile page that says "Add profile section". When you click on it, scroll to "Intro" and click "Looking for a new job".

A screen will open up that allows you to customize your work preferences, and also options for you to select who can see that you're open to opportunities. The two choices are: to let all of your network and recruiters with a #OpentoWork photo frame, and to only allow recruiters using LinkedIn Recruiter access it, while blocking recruiters at your current company.

6. **Improving SEO-** You can further improve search engine optimization by building on strongly relevant keywords in your professional headline, which is the title under your full name on the LinkedIn profile. Instead of writing something brief like "Strategic Account Manager", you can maximize it by populating

it with keywords like "Regional Strategic Account Manager- France, Benelux, North Africa at ABC Company | Lean Six Sigma Black Belt". These keywords will greatly improve SEO on search engines, as well as increase your search appearance on LinkedIn due to the keywords. You should also likewise pump up your job titles where relevant in your job experiences.

7. **Write a Summary**- There is a section at "Profile Strength" that allows you to create a summary. Summary is the first thing that recruiters look at when viewing LinkedIn profiles. Here, you can consider to populate it with important and relevant keywords which will put you in good light and gear you towards the opportunities you are aspiring towards.

8. **Join Professional Groups**- By joining professional groups, especially those which are related to your work, skillsets and industry, it gives you more legitimacy to get acquainted with people within that network, as well as to increase your visibility to your targeted audience when you write posts or make comments.

9. **The Comment on Comments Strategy**- Within the LinkedIn group you are in, whenever someone make a post, there is bound to be comments made by other people within that community. Since this group is going to be your likely target audience, you will be able to attract attention from other users of this same group to

your profile by doing so. One of the best ways to raise visibility, especially towards target user you try to establish connections with, is to first track this person down to the group of interest, and search for posts and comments made by him or her.

What you would then proceed to do is to comment on his or her comment, to make that person take notice of you. Do not say inane things like "great post" or "I agree with you", but try to put some thoughts into crafting an intelligent comment, one that can add value to the person, the poster or the group, in a way that does not make you look like a showoff, but rather an interesting professional.

10. **The Congratulatory Strategy**- Nothing better to say? At least you can start congratulating people. Look out for any notifications of high value connections you have who are starting new positions, or celebrating work anniversaries. There is a good chance that this high value connection will have other similarly high value connections noticing his or her profile update. Send congratulations to that person, with additional positive affirmative message that put you on the same level as this person, or to suggest a possibly close relationship (even though it may not be really the case). To give you an example, you can put something like, "Congratulations Gary! I am happy this is working out for you." Most of the person's connections who see this comment may assume that you are of the same high value and start paying attention.

11. **The Hashtags Strategy**- You can use hashtags extensively within LinkedIn to either market your profile, or search for specific term of interest. Start to find what are the common hashtags that your ideal target connection will be interested in. Go to the search bar and search for those hashtags, then look at the list of posts that pertain to these hashtags. Get in and start commenting on the comments or posts they make. Your aim here is to be able to get second to third-degree connections to take note of you.

12. **Caveat Emptor**- While you want to take full advantage of the power of LinkedIn, you should be reminded of one thing, that LinkedIn is not Facebook. Do not treat it like any other social media platform and start getting too personal or casual, making pointless posts and engage in unprofessional rants (like politics, etc). Those things will likely make professionals disrespect you, and since it is on social media, your folly may go viral and spread to many networks. Lately, I've also seen an increasing number of users who went all out posting, openly asking for jobs on the public network. I'd advice all the readers to not go down this route, because it greatly devalues the person in the eyes of others, where they find such behavior desperate, indiscrete, unprofessional and foolish, and will not respect such posters. Because if the professional is any good or competent, he or she will not stoop to committing such acts.

LinkedIn Recommendations, Endorsement and Shills

Most of the readers are probably familiar with the "Recommendations" section on LinkedIn. In case you didn't know already, this feature allows the connections within the person's LinkedIn network to provide testimonials on his or her professional competency, proficiency and other good words.

Under this section, there's a "Received" tab and a "Given" tab. "Received" tab consists of a list of testimonials given by the connections with the excerpts of their comments displayed. The "Given" tab consists of a list of testimonials that the profile owner give to their connections, also with excerpts.

You, as the profile owner can choose to "recommend" the connection by providing a testimony to this person, or ask for one by sending "ask for a recommendation" to request the person to write one for you.

The beauty of this feature is that it really makes the profile look wholesome when you have several connections provide you recommendations, because this will attest to how good a professional you are. As hirers and recruiters frequently trawl LinkedIn for suitable candidates, such profile will certainly make you stand out and increase the eligibility and therefore confidence in you.

But surprisingly, while this feature critically plays a role in greatly increasing the chances of interests and opportunities, I often find many LinkedIn profiles that are barren of any recommendations. I suspect that these LinkedIn users are probably too complacent, do not see a need in having this in their profile, or perhaps expecting someone to place a genuine testimony at some point.

Smart people who care about their profession would not slip up on such valuable opportunity though. They will proactively build up the "Recommendations" section on their profiles.

Most people who are proactive but unwise, will go all out to ask for recommendations from their network. And sometimes, they may get the recommendations they so desire. However, if I ever come across any profiles with long list of recommendations on "Received" tab and nothing on "Given" tab, I'll automatically assume this person to be a selfish, exploitative piece of crap. Those who are wiser and with better conscience will instead try to establish this in a more transactional manner with their connections, by getting help from fellow "shills".

These "shills" are people you've worked with, or interacted with, and happen to be on your LinkedIn network. Provided that you have or had a decent work relationship with them, or have been amicable with them, there's no reason why you should not ask them for help. Do not see the word "shills" in a negative light here, you're really taking steps to ask them to help one another to improve professional profiles together and furthermore, I trust that you are not asking them to write false accounts of your professional relationships (but that's entirely up to you).

The most straight forward way of doing so it is to "ask for recommendations" to the connection and also drop a message telling them that you'll always do the same for this connection, so as to help each other out. Do not send recommendations to the person first, but tell him or her that you're almost done with writing one.

Chances are, this request will be more agreeably executed upon than simply asking for recommendations without providing benefits to the other party. When you get the recommendations that you requested, please reciprocate in kind within reasonable time. This way, you'll instill confidence in your network to more willingly shill for you.

There's yet another important section within LinkedIn where you can also get your friendly shills to help you along. And that is with the "Skills & Endorsements" section. This feature allows the connections to click and endorse the different types of "Industry Knowledge" and "Other Skills" terms which are defined by the LinkedIn users. Say a LinkedIn user put up one of his skill as "Social Networking": when one of the connection clicks on it, it will show up under the "Skills & Endorsements" section with 1 endorsement. If 5 other connections click and endorse this same skill, the "Social Networking" skill button will register 6 endorsements. By having different skills endorsed, the profile will show an array of skill buttons with their appropriate labels and the number of endorsements; the more the better. These are very important, because they serve as the KEYWORDS which are used by prospecting recruiters and hirers to identify and match with their job descriptors during their candidate search. The wise LinkedIn user will customize and tailor these keywords to attract the kind of interests they hope to achieve with their visitors and prospective hirers.

Creating Your
Own Recommendation Letters

In order to verify the validity as well as your competency of your previous work experiences, many (but not all) hirers will probably request the candidate to provide some references from previous co-workers who were either direct supervisors or senior colleagues you've worked with. While this practice is certainly made to clear doubts (remember, I mentioned before that it's a factor in their reading of the Eligibility of the candidate), it may sometimes not work in favor of the candidates. Here is why.

The references are supposed to serve as testimonies for the candidates at the previous work place, but there are very few instances of an employee leaving the previous organization on good terms. Ex-supervisors may remain cordial to keep up the professional image towards the outgoing employee in those last few days at the organization, sometimes even behaving positively so.

But the reality usually warrants cynical afterthoughts- the ex-boss has a very strong likelihood of harboring resentment against this person for leaving, especially if the departure from the department incurs additional stress and problems at work in the worker's absence. The same may be applied to other senior ex-colleagues for the same reasons.

Some candidates who are conscious and concerned about such possibilities may politely ask them for references in which they will oblige out of basic courtesy. But what happens during the actual conversation between the hirer and the ex-boss or colleague may turn out to be a bit of a wild card.

Most references, who agree to help out this candidate will usually be obliged to try to say something positive about this person, but since the hirers will also tend to ask if there's also other comments concerning the weakness of the candidate, the references often take this opportunity to exact revenge, by hinting to the person's incompetency or use back handed compliments that do not put the person in a good light.

There may also be other problems associated with providing of references. If the references used are with ex-colleagues from previous organizations before the last one, the hirers will usually grow more skeptical towards the candidate, casting doubt in their heads that the last stint was probably a bad one. Another problem happens if the references cannot be contacted, for various reasons like invalid contact details, which will have the candidates trying to scramble for other possible allies.

In order to mitigate all these potential risks, the wise candidates may want to consider the use of recommendation letters. You see, the references may come and go, but recommendations always stay in your CV. Recommendation letters are good, because they may sometimes stop the hirers from seeking out references if they make the candidates sound good enough. Recommendation letters are useful, but not always a rule, and due to the inconvenience of drafting out a page, the ex-colleagues may not readily provide one for the candidate. And if they do commit themselves to write up one, it may not be one that is ideal enough for the candidate's preference. The solution to all of the above is to actually take a more proactive approach- which is to prepare the recommendation letters yourself.

You see, when you write up your own recommendation letter, you have full control over the content, and to greater personal satisfaction. As you do up one, you would want to write this document with the company's letterhead, so as to create a sense of legitimacy to the hirer, and also include the ex-boss or colleague's name and title while leaving a space for them to sign and maybe stamp with the company chop.

Before your last day, you'd request the person to simply just sign if off. Even if the person wants to edit it with own comments, he or she will not alter the content too drastically out of maintaining the magnanimity and professionalism in the relationship. They'll also more readily agree to doing this because it doesn't demand too much of their time.

With this recommendation letter in hand, you can evince the impression that you've received good testimony and endorsement, and most importantly, to create the impression that you've left the previous job on good terms. As a rule of thumb, try not to include contact details when possible, unless necessary, especially if you know that you left the company on bad terms. And if you want to go one step ahead of everyone else, you can even provide a contact detail that is invalid, so that the hirers will never get to the person; chances are they will not bother, but if they do, you can just tell them that you are not able to find the contact details.

If you already left the job without a letter, you can still try to do this retrospectively, by sending the same letter to the ex-colleagues or bosses and have them signed up, preferably in their presence (try to get them out for coffee one day and hand the letter to them to simply sign it up) than over email, because they'll probably not get back to you by email.

Bringing LinkedIn to Resumes

I previously talked about the use of recommendation letters in the building of your resume, which is a good way to minimize the risk associated within the conversations between the hirer and the reference. But there's no stopping you from going further to build more recommendations for your resume. What I'll suggest the jobseekers to do, when crafting the resume, is to take the power of LinkedIn beyond the internet by linking up the LinkedIn recommendations to your resume.

The whole purpose of this exercise, just like the crafting of recommendation letters, is to stop the assessors of your resume from asking too many questions, while positively influencing their decision to consider you. LinkedIn is a platform which primarily attract recruiters and hirers who are actively searching for candidates, and sure, having recommendations on a profile is certainly an "attractor" which works towards the benefit of the user. However, you have to understand that there's a certain disconnect between what people who are prospecting candidates look at, and what the people staring at resumes look at. If your resume is received by the hirer when you apply for jobs, particularly if it is not applied through LinkedIn, there's a good chance that the person who read your resume will not be looking at your LinkedIn profile, and those LinkedIn recommendations.

Most of the good stuffs are on LinkedIn and it contains more than what the resume offers. Regrettably, the job seekers do not understand that all the good stuffs on LinkedIn will not make it to the eyes of the hirers who read the resumes, which is a pity, because these good stuffs may critically influence the decision-making of the hirers. There is only so much that can be conveyed through the resume, but what if you're able to reconcile the two different platforms?

Most people assume that putting hyperlink that links to LinkedIn profiles on the resume is good enough. I beg to differ. In my opinion, many hirers, especially those working in large organizations seldom have time to peruse all the minute details on the resumes. They can certainly miss out on the hyperlink altogether. And what if the resume is a physical paper copy? The hyperlink will be rendered useless.

The best way to do this is to simply copy and paste the very good stuffs- the LinkedIn recommendations made by the user's connections into the resume. Do cite the LinkedIn source and include the full address to the LinkedIn profile (and yes you can hyperlink it up). Always state the name, title and company of the person who recommended you. If there's space limitation, it is possible to turn the recommendations into excerpts, while giving the excuse for the hirers to read more on your LinkedIn profile. You might want to keep all LinkedIn recommendations to a separate page from the main resume, which you want to limit to just one page, where you can draw attention to the hirer by mentioning that the recommendations are attached on the following page at the bottom of the resume.

Improving Your Resumes

Resumes (or CV- Curriculum vitae) are tools which are used as active means for your job application processes. If the hirers and the recruiters are the gatekeepers to the front gate of job opportunities, then the resumes are tools to influence the gatekeepers to open the gate. And in order to influence them, it has to turn into the key that unlocks the barriers put up by them.

The resumes are a summary of your career, which highlights your work experiences, education and skillsets, but are actually more than that. It needs to be constantly tailored to the different expectations of the job opportunities as well as the companies. The resume which you've used for the last job may not be applicable to the new job you're applying to.

On top of updating the job experiences you had, it has to be written in a way to fit into the new context of the target opportunity. The applicants should make effort to rewrite the resume to the next hirer. As a rule of thumb, it should look like something which matches the new job requirement. Below are several points for your consideration.

1. **Regarding Cover Letters**- Is it always necessary for the applicant to include a cover letter? Not really, unless it is requested by the job poster or hirer. As a

general rule, do not include any cover letter unless it's necessary. Most of the gatekeepers who receive applications do not have all the time in the world to look at paragraphs upon paragraphs in a document, much less so when there are hundreds of job applications. But if they do request for one, it is always prudent to be conscious about what is going to be inside the cover letter.

My advice is to keep it simple and straight forward, and to avoid any flowery proses, confusing narratives and long paragraphs. What you'd like to put in should be clear and precise to the reader. Highlight keywords relevant to the descriptor, suggest that you are a good fit, and then make yourself seem like the solution to address potential pain points of the department (while not putting down the company's capability, rather make yourself seem like someone who can bring additional benefits). Put several key messages in point forms and bold/underline when necessary.

2. **The Use of Keywords and Selling Yourself**- Almost all recruiters vet their candidates almost entirely based on keywords initially. If the keywords match the job expectations, they will then be considered. The resume is a document to sell yourself. It is important to list a short, simple summary highlighting the key points early in the document, and should contain keywords pertaining to the job descriptor, how your past experiences have culminated enough to handle the role, and how you are capable of contributing more,

you know, all the compelling reasons why you are the most suited to the role. I'd suggest that you include this section early just immediately after your brief bio specs (name, addresses, contact), and before you list your work experiences. This summary will capture the interest of the reader at first glance. Later, at the list of work experiences, do the same thing by highlighting what you do in the company, and how your work has benefited the organization.

3. **Keep to One Page**- You should try to keep the resume to one page when possible. Make it short and to the point. Most recruiters/hirers tend to frown upon long resumes and are less likely to want to read them, or will miss out details even if they do so. This one page will contain your bio specs (keep them simple, and if you can put them in the header, even better), followed by the summary with the keywords, job experience (position title, company and period), with the most important contributions highlighted, followed by a brief list on education, and a short section on other achievements, skills, awards.

Your point is to make it easy to read, and easy to manipulate and edit by the person who receives your resume. By enabling ease in their work, they will appreciate you much better. If you have cover letter, recommendation letters and other documents, keep them separate from the resume. If you're linking up recommendations from LinkedIn, keep them on a separate page as well.

4. **Regarding Photos**- As a general rule, do not include photos when possible, especially when you're a woman. The reason being that most HR hirers and recruiters are women, and they tend to subjectively apply their biases and prejudices, and it will definitely not help if the photo shows an attractive woman. My view on this is extremely cynical, but usually correct most of the time, so my advice is not to take the risk in this preliminary selection process.

5. **Give Mobile Friendly Documents**- There are times when your resumes are read on the go, via mobile devices. Most people put their resumes in word and pdf documents, which is generally acceptable. But in case you're using other format, or a dated version of such documents, do take note that it may not be readily accessed via the mobile phone. Try to open up your resume with your phone and see if it's accessible and readable. If it is not, you might want to transfer content to a mobile friendly document.

6. **Do Not Sound Negative**- Sometimes people are tempted to write negative things (which they may not be conscious of), concerning reasons why they leave their jobs, especially for short stint. Do not ever fall into that and write about getting terminated, or having problem with the organization. It will certainly reflect badly on the applicant. Rather, just keep to highlighting what you've contributed there, and not give away any reasons why you left the job.

7. **Make Your Resume Stands Out**- Let's get into the psychology of selection: in the sea of vast amounts of resumes, they kind of look like one another despite having vastly different content. Most of the resumes are on vertical page format. What if you can turn your resume sideway, into a horizontal page format? There's a good chance that it will stand out, and catch the interest of the hirer.

Another thing is the use of color. In the seas of black and white, some color will also stand out. But do be conscious of one thing, do not make the resumes too ostentatious or it will surely backfire. Because you have to remember that the resumes at the end of the day reflects your worth and respectability in the job market, and if it's too colorful, frilly, flashy or fluffy, it will not be deemed professional.

2. The Job Hunt

It's every man for himself in the brutal jungles of the employment market. This is where most of the excitement and dreadfulness of the job hunting is found, the actual HUNT.

When a jobseeker partakes in the hunt, he or she is doing so against other hunters with the same objectives of securing the best game, like participating in a non-fatal version of the Hunger Game, where at the end there can only be one who will emerge winner.

The jobseeker may have done all the homework and preparations, and armed with exemplary profile and qualifications, but as you know, seldom does the best job goes to the most qualified. While getting sufficiently prepared can certainly increase your chances of securing a job, the jobseeker need to also learn how to hunt for jobs (and subsequently sell yourself to the employers), instead of building resume.

Those who got the job get there due to a combination of prowess, resourcefulness and sheer luck, and hardly because of they are the most "qualified".

Many jobseekers would have already been seeking recourse for their unsatisfactory job hunts in most times, but this time round, the going actually gets tougher with the emergence of the Covid-19 pandemic. We're talking about massive unemployment that is currently taking place at unprecedented scale and rate across every parts of the world. Graduates and workers who are laid off are going to find themselves difficult to secure new jobs. The jungle is infested with hunters, but there are barely any games in sight. The extreme scarcity of visible opportunities is an extreme course of concern for all jobseekers in such unfortunate times.

However, this predicament may not so readily affect those jobseekers who are able to think and act differently from everyone else. And they who think and act differently will also likely see and find opportunities that are not in sight of many. I even daresay this type of jobseekers will likely survive any situations even with this Covid-19 pandemic, probably even thrive in it.

Because these demanding times presents some of the best opportunities for those who can that spot that sliver of hidden glitter from the dark heavy clouds of doom and doom while the rest are probably too fixated in the darkness of mediocrity. The majority of the jobseekers will still use old knowledge to try to find new opportunities, even when situation demands strategic updates. They stick to the same old routine of job search based on how they used to do it in the past, which they probably grew too complacent with or had taken for granted, due to the ease of finding them (usually with clicks of buttons on job boards). Sadly speaking, most opportunities tend not to go to this group of people, but to the wily and resourceful few.

In this chapter, we talk about the many things that are not mentioned by other books on similar subjects. I will bring up grim truths and realities of the employment market, which is one that is already full of deceit and entrapment even during better times, from the point of view as a market insider. I will also share with the job seekers novel strategies and tactics in finding opportunities in the most unimaginable of places.

Currently, most of the jobseekers are probably familiar with job search in the most fundamental sense. Like, if you want to apply for jobs in the most straight forward and easiest way, you'd probably send your resumes through job boards or company websites

You've probably had some dealings with recruitment agents who had work on your behalf to link you up with prospective employers. And I trust that all the readers are familiar with using keywords to search for the opportunities of interest, either on search engines or in job portals.

If you know all the above, you'll have no problem understanding most of this chapter, and most importantly, getting valuable information here which will put you far ahead of most of the other average job seekers out there.

Be Different and Creative

Mediocre by definition means of only average quality. But everyone of us who have heard and used this term before probably felt it more negatively than how it is defined. To call someone mediocre makes that person seem less than average. And in many aspects of business, investments and career, the mediocre occupies the large part in the middle of the Gaussian curve. This is an area of purgatory, which can be worse than hell due to it turning foul with most of the masses therein, stupefied and stagnated.

I do not mean to insult any person as mediocre, but to use it as a metaphor for the masses which it represents in this area. A more insulting term for people who straddle this area is probably sheeple, and most people are sheeple unfortunately.

The sheeple follow one another, taking similar paths and making similar decisions, with similarly predictable behavior and outcome. Most of the sheeple lack critical thinking, because they tend to think in the same unquestioning manner like everybody else. In terms of the job search, they will use the same technology, believe in the narratives by the authority and follow the methods of the popular gurus.

In every job search, they will represent one another's greatest competition, unaware of the fact that they cost their own chances of securing any jobs, because they are all applying to the same job postings, using the same methods of application, and are liable to face similar outcomes. The competitions are tremendous over this one job that everyone is vying for. This phenomenon had been especially evident with the advent of technology like job boards, in place of traditional methods of classified ads. The job boards are easy to access, and easy to use, where anyone with internet access can just send the resume over with a click of the button.

In the past, the hiring manager will probably receive a dozen job applicant letters in a week from the classified job ads. These days, they are overwhelmed with influx of hundreds upon hundreds of applications flooding their inboxes from the the job board adverts.

Because of the huge surfeit of applications, there's a strong likelihood that most of them will not be properly read. The hiring managers will mostly just skim through headlines randomly, from the few resumes that are actually read. Most of the applications may not even be read. Naturally, when you combine all the factors above, the odds against getting a job are exponentially increased, for those people who choose such course of application. And sadly, this is the only way most job seekers know how to do their job search in the current age.

I've mentioned before that the most qualified don't get the jobs. Jobs will tend to go to a person who is able to find the right opportunity, able to get to the right person, and able to sell themselves. Otherwise, the person is just plain lucky. In order for our dear readers to secure a better chance of securing jobs, it is best not to be mediocre like the sheeple-who are mostly the rest of the other fellow job seekers planning for the same endeavor you are undertaking.

Remember, you do not want to be in the majority middle. Rather, you increase your success rates of securing a job by looking at where the rest fail to look, getting your resume to the key person with unorthodox methods, making your resume stand out from the other applications, and selling yourself in a way which will seal the deal. Be the contrarian. Be different and creative in your approach, and rid yourself of the unhelpful and unsuccessful mediocrity, by starting to aim for the extreme outliers, come hell or high water, which is essentially what this chapter will bring you to.

Caveat emptor: yet there should be a limit to where you can go with "different and creative", and you will find out more when I discuss about guerrilla job hunting tactics later in the chapter.

Revisiting the Pareto Principle

During my time as employee in various careers, I often come across this corporate speak about the 80/20 rule, echoed extensively in the more commercial side of the business. It's even a bit of a "sensational" lingo to drop in the office by people who feel smug about it. Essentially, this smarty-pants concept talks about a rule which finds that 20% of the clients/customers generate 80% of the revenues, and therefore 20% should be worked on more attentively.

It is also seen as a concept where you minimize effort to focus on what is more critical to achieve maximum results, although the sales manager would not want this to get to his subordinates. So the concept was further twisted by those sales managers to suggest a salesperson may get a positive outcome for every 5 leads worked upon, thus justifying that the salespeople should work on as many leads as possible, in multiples of 5.

That 80/20 rule is known as the Pareto Principle, a concept especially popular in the corporate circles, and it is essentially an observation that often a small amount of inputs (like 20%) is responsible for the large majority of the output (the 80%). It is not a hard and fast rule but many followers do take it literally.

In the world of career advices, many experts also often stress on the importance of the Pareto Principle. They mentioned that only 20% of the jobs that you spend your time on and apply for will bring you 80% of the success rate (phone interviews, interviews and in turn, offers), and the candidates should therefore look for those 20% and put more effort in getting them. That means for every 10 job opportunities you encounter, you prioritize and then fixate on 2 of them to be your precious 20% to work on. Those 20% generally should be based on factors such as:

1. Selection criteria matching your background

2. Culture fit looking like it fits your personality

3. Something you could be passionate/excited about

And when you have decided on the roles you have most chance of obtaining, you can use the extra time to be more strategic in your attempts to secure them (the so-called experts will usually ask the person to tediously fill in their specially designed (and patented) worksheets with many columns in order to get the person to work on a more "strategic approach" on the 20% that matters):

1. Keep a list of every specific job you are applying for

2. Tailor your resume to match each of those specific jobs

3. Create a cover letter with bullet points reflecting why you match their specific criteria

4. On your list, create a column to remind you to follow up regularly (once a week often recommended) to find out the progress of your application

Once you have created your list and used your additional time more efficiently, you will have a lot more time to spend on other areas of your job search including:

1. Updating your LinkedIn profile and connecting with appropriate contacts

2. Attending networking events specific to your field of work

3. Joining appropriate networking groups on LinkedIn

4. Approaching companies directly who may not necessarily have advertised, but who you think could benefit from your skill set (author: this suggestion by them is actually pretty good, I do talk about this one in the book)

All of the above seems like a good idea. Yes, focusing on the 20% that matters may really increase your chances of securing a job. But what happen to the other 80% of the jobs out there? Are they to be disregarded altogether? Additionally, the danger of the fixation of a 20% may lead to what is known as the "sunk cost fallacy", whereby a person continually sticks with a decision (and usually one which does not seem to bear fruit) because much time and effort have already been invested and want to make sure it isn't lost.

The grouse with the so-called business consultant/job gurus who espoused the Pareto Principle is that they only superficially know the textbook formula but do not know the full nature of this concept. Nassim Taleb, a Lebanese-American essayist, scholar, mathematical statistician, former option trader and risk analyst, and author of widely acclaimed books like "The Black Swan", explained that the Pareto Principle is not as straight forward as you think: "If there is inequality, then those who constitute the 20 percent in the 80/20 rule also contribute unequally" and it might as well be a "50/1 rule if the 50% of the work comes from 1% of the workers".

It could be that one person within that pool of 20% does all of it. Or half of it. It doesn't matter. If there is inequality, then those who constitute the 20 percent in the 80/ 20 rule also contribute unequally— only a few of them deliver the lion's share of the results.

Thus, if you have a jobs list where 20% of the employers generate 80% of the successes you might decide to jettison the 80% of the job list that generate only 20% of the successes and keep only the 20% that are the biggest success contributor. Taleb's point is that now you probably have an 80/20 ratio again with 20% of the remaining opportunities generating 80% of the remaining good outcomes.

*While the Pareto principle is costly during applications, it can be applied when you try to maneuver for successive interview (after the first), mitigate delays and reverse objections. It may be worthy to invest more efforts in chances towards closure.

Increase Your Chances
With Barbell Strategy

In this section, I'd actually take the liberty to encourage my dear readers to take on some responsible risks. This statement may draw flak and puzzlement, as it can seem rather confusing and confounding to the average person, because the average job seekers are seeking jobs precisely to ensure job security, which is wholly antithetical to the notion known as "risk".

But these risks that I am talking about is meant to increase the chances of success, particularly for job hunting, and which will not cause any damage to the individual. The only risk that will happen is increased difficulty in getting certain jobs. What exactly am I advocating then, one might ask?

Before I talk about such risks, I want the readers to know well my intent and persuasion here, which is to get a person up for contrarian mindset, to think ahead and differently from what the general masses (sheeples) are thinking. Because, if you follow conventional norm, you'll either end up in mediocrity, or in the case of job search, landing no successful outcome. The risks that I propose you to take, while harder to achieve, may actually increase your chances with getting more promising results in your job search. Does this seem even more confusing? Read on.

Now let's go back to the sheeples. We know this herd-like behavior of the masses. They follow their lives in the band in the middle, and will likely follow one another and do predictably the same things. In the case of job hunting, they will probably all land up at the same jobs, increasing the competition, leading to over-application for the same opportunity, and all of them losing out this opportunity to one person.

Risk management on the other hand, allows a person to not fall within the range of mediocrity, but increase successes through taking measured, responsible risks. Now, we're getting close to it, but let's look at the Pareto Principle and Nassim Taleb in retrospection, as well as some novel strategy from the latter.

The 80/20 Pareto Principle is a good start for something interesting, but it has its flaws, and the sunk cost fallacy might actually propel and sink the job seekers into higher risks bordering some danger- from wasted time and resources, negligence of other opportunities, emotional damage resulting from obsessive compulsion and disappointment, to jeopardizing relationships with targeted organization due to the overzealous approach.

I'd suggest the readers to take a leaf from risk management experts like Nassim Taleb, who have critically examined unforeseen events termed "black swan events" and its effects on the majority vs individuals who are more "anti-fragile" (those who may stay resilient or even benefit from such events). According to him, failure is a far more common experience than success in the "fat-tailed" world we're living in, and in order to protect oneself from unforeseen or unexpected negative events and avoid hindsight bias, it is possible to take up risk strategies like the "Barbell Strategy", since we're not able to forecast sudden shock and surprises.

Simply put, the barbell strategy involves taking an extremely defensive attitude and excessively aggressive attitude at the same time, while holding no middle-ground. Taking the middle way is only an illusion of safety. You're still exposed to potentially ruinous events, with no chance of the unlimited upside that also swirls out of the same chaos.

In a barbell strategy, the person will target two extremes of the spectrum at once, while the middle, as little as possible. In effect, you want to avoid the purgatory of mediocrity in the middle of the Gaussian curve and settle for the two outliers at the extremes. One end, with highest risk and highest reward, and the other end, lowest risk and lowest reward.

If a person like the idea of 80/20, not in the pure Pareto Principle sense, he or she can possibly use it too, without giving up on the 80% that's it. The simplest example can be illustrated with an investment portfolio: Invest 80% of your portfolio in dull, risk-free assets, but allocate the remaining 20% to aggressive investments. That is much better than investing all your money in average-risk assets. And it leaves you with a far more robust portfolio.

Supposing you lost your 20% in the aggressive investments, you still have 80% of safe assets to back you up. But if you make money from the aggressive 20%, the payout will be much more handsome, perhaps many folds more than what the average person invests in.

Similarly, this strategy can be applied across jobs and career. Let's first look at career development. The perfect "horizontal" barbell strategy job is one that is stable, secure and easy on one extreme (80%), while on the other end, the pursuit of highly risky and speculative side projects (20%).

That stable job should have few intellectual demands and high job security, the kind that won't weigh in on your mind the moment you leave the office. The rest of the time, you're free to pursue your side hustle. If your big dreams don't work out, you still have a regular income source to keep working towards financial independence. If your big dreams work out, you can plan to ease out your day job, which brings us to the "vertical" barbell strategy.

In the vertical barbell model, you spend a chunk of time focused on accumulating wealth and security through a regular job, then the next spell single-mindedly focused on your dream side hustle. You can do this by alternating between the secure jobs and the side hustle in a serial fashion, perhaps taking different terms (in and out of the two of them) to see if the speculative gig pays off. These models have brought about financial freedom (or the freedom from employer enslavement) to many people who diligently followed its formula.

Now let's finally touch on the job hunting side of things. I've adopted this strategy and came up with two ways you can use them. The first way you can apply the barbell strategy is on the choice of jobs, based on growth and challenges. This part may be skewed accordingly to the ambitions and appetites of the job seekers, but I believe that generally, most job seekers are more inclined and open to take on some challenges to develop their career.

On one extreme end, you should aim for opportunities that are highly attractive, above your caliber and which will demand you to get out of your comfort zone to grow and encompass more skillsets. The upside is career progression, glamor and fat check if you get it. The easiest way to find such opportunity is to look for one which will be a next step up from your last level. If you're particularly ambitious, this part should consist of 80% of the opportunities you are applying to, to increase your wager.

On the other extreme end, you should aim for jobs that you have absolute mastery and even advantage over the rest, where you will have the capacity to be on top of the game and get highly valued in that department based on your past experiences, perhaps even slightly overqualified for it. The upside is increased likelihood of employment and security. This part should constitute 20% of the opportunities you are applying to, if you are the more ambitious sort.

Avoid the middle-ground, which is a lateral parallel of your last position you had with the same demands and challenges; such positions are where you'll find most of your similarly leveled industrial counterparts flock to. My suggestion also, do not overexert efforts on the 20% or 80% at either ends (do not follow the Pareto Principle), but treat them with equal measures of your time and effort during application.

The second way you can apply the barbell strategy is targeting the easiest and hardest to find jobs. The point of going for the hardest, is that if the processes are more difficult, it's also less likely for the other job seekers to find, which will decrease your competition significantly. On one end there's what I term the "hidden job market", which demands creative ingenuity and strategies/tactics to get into. This segment is usually off-access to most people, but I'll be covering this later in the chapter, teaching the readers how to tap into them. This can constitute 20% of the opportunities you are seeking.

On the other end of the spectrum is the easiest and least risky way of job application, which is to directly send resumes through job boards or company websites. This one is a no brainer that should not trouble you too much, and constitute the majority of the job applications you employ, in the range of the 80% in frequency. Equal time must be spent while applying to both 20% and 80%. Unlike the Pareto Principle, you do not overemphasize on that 20% to avoid sunk cost fallacy.

And then there's the middle-ground to be avoided or minimized- the use of recruitment agents. While requiring more effort than simply sending resumes over the internet, this is actually the cesspool for the mediocre, especially during trying times like Covid because they thought their chances will be increased with a little help by another person. The unsuspecting herd will flock to this middle solution, and unbeknownst to them, this middle solution frequently contributes to the most disappointments in the job search.

Use the Right Technology

Job seekers in this day and age are spoilt for choice, due to the great amount of technology at their disposal. Yet this presents a problem, because the information overload on the internet makes it difficult to discern proper use of the right technological tools.

There was a time when job boards were seen as revolutionary. Websites like Monster, lived up to its name by growing into a monstrous job board of epic proportion. It was the first name people referred to when they decided to start browsing for opportunities. The job seekers could search through different industries, sectors and categories for all kinds of job functions, titles and terms at the ease of clicks on the internet. The website made its presence felt internationally, and became the ultimate go-to even to this date.

And then came increasingly large numbers of Monster competitors and other job boards vying for different niches. Some became equally monstrous in size, like CareerBuilder, others became specialized in their particular niches like AngelList for startup jobs, FlexJobs for flexible/remote jobs, Upwork/Fiverr for freelance jobs and Nurse.com, exclusively for nurse jobs.

The game changers came in subsequent waves. The most famous undoubtedly being LinkedIn, which is probably one of the most popular job search site by now. Starting as just a social media platform for professionals, it grew to become increasingly like a Facebook for professionals, but also taking on features of the job boards. There are many features that can be used for the average job seekers, like connecting and interacting with other professionals and groups, from getting recommendations from other people to job recommendations in the dashboard, and of course applying to jobs and getting alerts as well.

Glassdoor also assumes position as another top job search site right now because it can give the jobseekers insights on the companies they are interested in, based on reviews of employees/ex-employees, and discover the salary ranges from the paymasters. Indeed is another top job board of monstrous proportion, especially in recent years, overtaking Monster's position since 2010, with its novel idea of aggregating job listings from thousands of job boards and websites into its platform. ZipRecruiter is the new kids on the block with its clever way of matching jobs with candidates, allowing the recruitment process to be shortened considerably.

Nowadays, all these job boards are even considered somewhat dated by modern standards (maybe with the exception of LinkedIn due to its constant innovations). But despite that, these job boards are the first places that every job seekers head to for job hunting. There are new job boards that try to be more creative, like creating referral programs for peer to peer users (ReferHire), and charging users to access exclusive, high paying jobs (The Ladders) but they are nowhere as close in proportion to some of the aforementioned "monsters". Almost every of these job boards allow the job seekers to do additional fancy things like uploading resumes and receiving job alerts in the emails and that seem good enough for the average users. I do not need to teach the readers how to use these websites and do keyword searches, since I trust that none of the readers here are new to these platforms.

Since we detest mediocrity, I would encourage the readers to be different from the sheeples, the unthinking majority who only know these few outlets. Job boards are great to go to, but you should also start taking advantage of available technology out there. Here are some of them (I do not include resume builders, because this chapter is about job hunting):

1. **Jobscan**- This software is built from algorithms used in top Applicant Tracking Systems (ATS). ATS are those nasty things implemented by companies to filter the candidates' resumes. What Jobscan can do is to match your resume with the job descriptor and determine the chances of it passing through the ATS.

2. **CareerExplorer**- This platform helps you find your ideal career by taking the career test. For those who are still trying to find themselves and undecided.

3. **Startwire/MixMax**- These tools allow the candidates to see the status of their job applications, to see if it had been received and read or left in the cold.

4. **SalesQL/ZoomInfo/RocketReach**- Need to contact certain person in an organization? Find this person's contact details to make connections with that person. The first one is a Chrome extension that allows you to pull contact details from LinkedIn and which I will cover in greater details later in the chapter. The other two allows you to find other people not on LinkedIn.

5. **PayScale**- Research on the most important part of a job, the salary. This platform allows you to search and compare through the different positions in the industry to make sure you're on the right track for negotiation or whether you're in the right salary range.

6. **Switch**- This mobile app is the "Tinder of online job searches," which allows the jobseekers to create a professional profile and upload their resume, then receive job recommendations which they can pursue or pass on with just a swipe. A right swipe sends a notification and an anonymous professional profile to the hiring manager. If the interest is mutual, a chat feature opens and the two can begin a conversation about next steps.

7. **LinkUp**- This is one of the purest job search engine out there, which only advertises verified positions that are up-to-date, sourced and gathered from company websites directly. No red herrings, pesky recruitment agents and phantom jobs (we'll talk about that soon).

Avoiding Phantom Jobs

The last thing you want to do in your hunt is to waste your valuable time on opportunities that may not even exist at all. These non-existent opportunities are what I term as "phantom jobs", and they are one of the most disgusting things to happen in the job market, because they usually exist for the purpose of deceit, although also rarely, could be a case of genuine omission.

And yet, despite their undesirable nature, they probably take up **more than half** of what is out there in the job market (primarily on job boards), which is astounding to say the least. It is sad that there are companies and organizations out there who has to resort to such underhanded hoax, and even more saddening only to find out that there's actually a sheer number of them who do such things on a regular basis, to prey on the gullibility of the job seekers. I'll explain the different types of phantom job postings and also point out that sometimes (although rarely) it may not be out of deliberation/deceit.

1. **Postings designed for future needs**- Some companies have frequent needs to fill job vacancies on a timely basis, as the result of a regular turnover. In some of these cases, these vacancies stretch across broad categories of jobs. As a result, these employers often advertise for such jobs before the openings

emerge, to secure a pipeline of qualified candidates that can be tapped in a hurry once the need arises.

2. **Postings designed for data collection-** On a more sinister note, phantom jobs may be advertised simply for the purpose of collecting resumes/data, without the intent of fulfilling near term prospects of job availability or of any sort of urgency. Perhaps the resumes may be used in the indeterminate future, but the profiles are also collected for building up databases and even studying market trends. The most culpable organizations are the recruitment agencies who do that all the time. Most of the job postings by recruitment agencies on job boards are phantom listings, and they tend to get away with it as the identity of the clients are not disclosed. They constitute as number one for all the phantom job listings found on job boards.

3. **Error postings-** Some jobs listed on job boards may have been filled, or halted (due to budget cut etc), but the board may not have been timely informed or caused a delay in the process, thus resulting in the jobs that are still erroneously been advertised despite its unavailability.

4. **Competing postings-** In some cases, the hiring company may have hiring needs in various areas, but only the budget to add a subset of these people. Once the aggregate hiring limit has been reached, the remaining job postings effectively become null and void. Applicants for the latter then will find that they have been seeking jobs that have vanished.

5. **Postings as a front for closed positions**- There are instances whereby certain positions are internally or informally filled (indeed, this correspond to 50% of the entire job market out there in what is known as the "hidden job market" which I'll discuss later) but public job postings are still required as a formality undertaken to comply with human resources department rules that mandate advertising of open positions. This is the second most common phantom job listing.

The next thing I'd like to share to the readers is on how to identify probable phantom job listings to avoid:

1. **Reposted jobs-** One of the most common practice of phantom job posters is reposting the same job posting after a certain period of time. From what I notice, it's usually about one month in between. When you come across any job posting, do a search by title and descriptor, and use duration option if available to see if this job had been posted before. If you find the same job posting had been made at least 3 times in the past 3-4 months, that's worthy of red flagging.

2. **Date of posting-** Another way of determining if a posting is a phantom job is to examine the date that the original advertisement was first posted. You may come across a new listing on a job board, and this post may direct you to the original advertisement on the company's website. If this new job posting is for an advertisement that had been around for more than 2 months, there's a chance that it's likely for a job that never was.

3. **Redirection and misdirection**- Say you come across a listing on a job board for company A, but the link for application brings you to nothing, or to a contact/landing page that does not suggest any relationship to company A, there could be something fishy. If you are brought to an "error 404", there's still the possibility of technical error on the part of company A, but if that application link brings you to a damned recruitment agency, it's another red flag here.

4. **Frequency of appearance**- Do you always come across that same job whenever you go into the job board, and/or across all the other job boards? Yes, you can red flag it too.

5. **Job postings by recruitment agencies**- While not all jobs posted by recruitment agencies are phantom jobs, there's a very strong likelihood that they are. Yes, your resumes count towards their database building, even for every genuine job that they posted. When they choose to be dishonest, they can do all kind of things because they cannot be apprehended: when they post on job boards, the identity of the clients they are working on are not disclosed, and they may even claim that they are working on highly confidential role to add to the whole aura of exclusivity. If you're bothered enough, you can copy the job descriptors and paste it on search engine- there's a good chance that you can then find out the company and position that they're either working on, or copied from.

Do Not Deposit
Resumes at Job Boards

Most job boards these days have this function which allows the job seekers to upload their resumes, to be deposited to the website's database. The idea behind this function is for the sake of easier application the next time round, and/or to increase the chances of the candidate's exposure to the companies/hirers who would go inside this database and look at these profiles. Functionally they make sense, but in reality, they can actually hurt the job seekers instead of help them.

Before we get to the bad part, let's first try to see what's the "more significant" point of this function. Sure, it does all those things that they promise, but more. Job boards, like all businesses need to make money, but they have already changed their business model many years ago when the market became extremely competitive.

They used to charge customers in the past for job listings with packages tiered at different prices, but these days, most of the popular job boards are already giving them the option to list jobs for free. The few ways the job boards can still make money are: featured listings- which are listings put in a more conspicuous location, or featured more frequently, advertisements- through banners and affiliate links, advertorials- where they are paid to write something good about products/customers, and lastly paid access to special sections. The resumes that are deposited/uploaded to the website are usually put in the special sections (database) that are only accessible to paying or high level customers. BUT, the resume database has increasingly lost its business relevance these days as most customers do not find it useful most of the time, which result in the customers not wanting to pay for this option, which lead to boards doing away with the fees for such access, in order to retain the customers.

Why is it not useful for the customers (the hirers/employers)? At the candidates/job seekers end, this function is always free for all. There's a tendency for more candidates, especially the weaker ones, to want to put up their resumes online. When you've a surfeit of poor quality candidates, no matter how good the other candidate is, his or her profile will be lost in the sea of mediocrity.

The customers who used to pay learnt their lessons when they found that most of the profiles within the database are mediocre and they have to wade through the immense mountain of crap to get to profiles that are suitable.

When they no longer have to pay for it, they will just go in for the sake of it when they run out of options. As the database already formed a negative connotation, every profile the customers chance upon, no matter how qualified, are tainted with the negative association. And mind you, these profiles have full information on the identity and sensitive information concerning the candidates. By the negative association, a decent candidate may be relegated to something lower.

And customers of job boards are not just HR/hirers of companies, but agents from other recruitment agencies. Indeed, these agents spend even more time than the rest on this database, because they need to gather every available resources they can to help them achieve/hit their targets (resumes are like the recruitment agents' commodities).

The real nightmare begins when the resumes of decent candidates get into the hands of the recruitment agents and get spammed across all the different organizations. Having your resume sent all over is not a good thing at all, and will certainly not increase your chances of getting a job. Instead, it will dilute your market value with repeated exposure to different places, because when your profile appears too often, the other party will tend to think negatively about you.

I will discuss at great lengths about how dangerous the recruitment agents can be for candidates in later topics.

Another danger of the resume database, a likely possibility (or probability), is that your profile and personal data can be sold for money. Every business that engage in some level of data collection is perfectly able to do so, and what is better than a rather complete data set of your curriculum vitae?

All things aside, there's a likelihood that if you merely attach your resume when you apply through the job listings on the board, even when you have not deposited your resume before, the system will still be able to capture your resume and automatically deposit it into the database without your permission. If you really want to play safe, make sure that the job listing direct you to the actual company career/job website, instead of applying to a listing through the inmail option within the job board. If you do not have this option, you should still able to know the company from the job listings, and then write directly with the email addresses of the relevant hirers/decision makers.

There is one exception to the rule though, and that is LinkedIn. It is comparatively safe to deposit/save resumes on this website, or to apply through the inmails in the job listings. The reason why you're able to do so on LinkedIn is because it has grown so large that almost every professional from all over the world are using it now and doing the exact same things like sending resumes to apply for jobs, and its network is not jam packed with majority of the mediocre demographics, hence minimizing the spread for overexposure and abuse.

Making Sense in the Age of Network Disaster

The whole pitch about the absolute importance of networking in job hunting belongs to the same outdated advices dispensed by "experts" who probably also argued the importance of the MBA. Networking (for job hunting that's it) is perhaps one of the most overrated and misused strategy that has a proven record of backfiring, causing absolute "network disaster" upon eager, impressionable and naive job seekers.

There are certainly merits that can be seen in some level of networking, particularly if the job seekers are having "actual professional networks" to begin tapping on. The insurmountable disaster that befalls the amateurs happens when they start connecting with strangers or making deeper connections with mere acquaintances in the work circles by treating network like a "numbers game".

Before we get to the bad, let's talk about the benefits of networking. The real purpose of networking is "professional support", in the career sense. Professional networks of a person are initially established and based on previous professional relationships with other people, within or outside the organization, as well as through acquaintances from similar industries. It is expanded to other people, based on recommendations by people already in the network, or initiated by people (or by the person) on the basis of common associations. It is expanded even further by connections who believe in the possibility of future relationships (e.g. a hiring manager connecting with a prospective candidate).

Through this network of people, is where the professional support is found, which the working professional can readily use it for two main purposes: a) to find help in getting things done, for example, like finding suitable business partnership, and b) to build political clout, either as just an image or as a working tool of power and contention.

In networking, the potency of influence lies in proven track records of competency and positive relationships. If the person has neither, then he or she can hardly exercise any influence over the network. Whereas on the other hand, the potency of the network itself lies in the quality of the connections. If the network is full of low level junior workers, it will be hard to get help for more senior career matters.

Networks are especially helpful for fostering new business partnerships. But relying networking to secure job opportunities can be a rather difficult task. Politics in the workforce can severely affect the network. Every industry counterpart in the network, no matter how close their personal relationship to the jobseekers are, are largely more concerned about their own well beings. That's the cynical reality of human nature. They would rather secure the job opportunities for themselves than the jobseekers. Sometimes they do it out of courtesy, but they will tend to only recommend jobs that they've no chance of succeeding with.

Similarly, no matter how close a relationship a jobseeker can foster with someone in the network, he or she will never truly know what the person really thinks of the jobseeker. If someone in the network secretly hates the jobseeker, he or she can take advantage of the situation by sabotaging the career prospects and image of this person within the community, after find out the jobseeker's desire to get a job.

And how about finding jobs through more senior contacts than similar counterparts? Well, as I've mentioned earlier, the strength and potency of the jobseeker really counts on proven track records of competency. The senior contacts themselves who did not have previous working relationship with the jobseekers may not know enough or doubt the ability of the jobseekers, especially if they are total strangers.

Total strangers or people who roughly know you by your face, are not obliged to help, because they don't see the need to. The hundreds of them may have accepted your request for connections on LinkedIn, but you cannot expect them to stretch their bandwidth to assist your job recommendation request, because it is simply too troublesome to do so. The unfortunate thing about the whole "Networking" culture on LinkedIn has jobseekers taking this "groundbreaking" idea too literally and reach out every of their connections for jobs. Worse still, in recent years, when LinkedIn has morphed into a career Facebook of sorts, where the jobseekers can actually write posts to all their connections, and openly ask for jobs in their posts! They may eventually get something, because some of their connections may want to take the opportunity (the power of social media!) to play the hero card and offer them some positions (usually menial ones) in order to get acclaims, but these posters are usually regarded extremely negatively due to their sheer audacity and desperation. The normal mind would rationalize that if they are so good, they need not go through such great lengths to ask for jobs.

If things can be so potentially bad, should the readers simply abandon the whole idea of networking then? Actually no, because networking is still a good tool for job prospecting if used appropriately and sensibly. Networking is actually one of the best ways for job seekers to get into what is known as the "hidden job market", which are jobs that are not advertised. Through the power of connections, this can be tapped into.

Most of us, quite frankly speaking, are not the best networkers. It takes a special breed, those thick-skinned, wheeler-dealer, hustler type to actively interact and grow their networks. We're usually quite contented to have those few in our small network list on social media, but not keen to go out and shake hands with everybody. My advice is, keep it that way, but you might want to start adding some people that matters to your list. There's no awkwardness in striking up conversations with this type of strangers, because these people would actually want to speak eagerly to you.

In order for the contacts to even want to share such hidden opportunities to the jobseeker, there must be some motivations for doing so. One of those people who can benefit from sharing hidden opportunities are- the recruitment agents. These people, sometimes known as executive search consultant, recruiters or headhunters, earn their commissions (and keep their jobs) by making placements of candidates for their clients and they happen to be my most favorite people to talk about and bash. I'd encourage the readers to use them, but only after you read what I've got to say about them, and learn how to use them wisely later in the chapter.

The second type of people you might want to consider adding are the potential hirers. Who are the potential hirers? Those people who post jobs on job boards and those people who ask the people to post jobs on their behalf to the job boards. Your prime targets are therefore, the HR manager who is in charge of recruitment, the key decision maker (or prospective boss), who is a head of a certain unit with job functions that match the descriptors in the job posts, and most IMPORTANTLY, people with "talent acquisition" in their title. All you need to do is to request connections with them. And then you can write them to ask if there are any job opportunities, and most of them are obliged to answer you as it is their duty to do. The "talent acquisition" person are even more than obliged to do so, because it is their job to talk to candidates.

Lastly, there's actually a pretty solid strategy that is frequently overlooked. Most of the networkers look forward to adding more people. But what they missed out on are people who are already in their network. I term the strategy: backward networking. When you network backwards, you are actually counting on the people that mattered in the past. Do you remember the supervisors who helped in your thesis, the former HR manager who helped you with securing your job, the ex-boss who is now in a different organization, or even your former senior ex-colleagues? Why not start reaching out to them, the people who had proven track record of helping you in the past. There's a chance that they will likely help you again.

Data Mining Through LinkedIn

Have you ever thought how good it will be if you can have direct email addresses of those people who matters in your job search? This can soon become a reality for you.

There's something which can be done on LinkedIn that most users don't know about. And that is, it's actually possible to export connections from the user's network into a list, which contains the person's contact details, including the email addresses! But since you now know about it, you can pat yourself on the back, because you are going to be way ahead of others in the game for the job search.

Most users on LinkedIn thought that the only way of communications with other connections is entirely restricted to the use of "Messaging" or through the LinkedIn Messenger, and thought that contact details are strictly off limits if the connection doesn't allow it to be shown (and yes, they usually won't).

Wouldn't it be good if you can write a formal email to the HR manager who seems to ignore your messages on LinkedIn? Well, it is now possible to get this information that you want. The easiest way to do it is by exporting data of your LinkedIn connections to a spreadsheet. However, there's always a catch, which I will also mention in a while.

Alright, go to LinkedIn, and click the "Me" icon at the top of your homepage. Select "Settings & Privacy" from the dropdown. Click "Data Privacy" on the left rail. Under "How LinkedIn uses your data" section, click "Change" next to "Get a copy of your data". Select "Want something in particular?" Select the data files you're most interested in. Select "Connections", then click "Request archive". Enter your password and click "Done". You will receive an email to your primary email address which will include a link where you can download your list of connections. This is written based on the 2020 workflow to date.

When you open the file (in csv format) on Excel, you will find the data consisting of your first-degree connections listed and categorized according to the data you wanted. But you'd be probably shocked by what you see- most of your contacts have missing fields under the "Email" column! Well, this happens for good reason, because LinkedIn users are given the option to not show their email addresses, which is understandably reasonable to do to protect the privacy of the users, and since LinkedIn respects the users' decisions, they will not show it even if you've exported the data. This happened after 2018; before that, you could pull all sorts of information off LinkedIn.

But thankfully there's actually ways to get around this. The method to madness lies in the use of third-party tools. There are actually all kinds of them, like **SignalHire**, **Dux-Soup** and **Improver** that will help you to pull email addresses from LinkedIn connections, but I will talk about a pretty good one, which is **SalesQL**, because it's largely free. In order to use it, you should have a Chrome browser. You'll download the

SalesQL extension and install in Chrome. Once it is done, you simply download the connections and get their email addresses. For the free versions, you're limited to a maximum of 100 connections per month, but do you know what you'll get? You can not only get contact details from first-degree connections, but also second and even third-degree connections! Yet, there's a caveat- it's best to limit to how many connections you do in a 24-hour period, as the software scans LinkedIn, and you wouldn't want to have issues with LinkedIn.

Beside these methods, there's also always the options to use RocketReach or ZoomInfo.

Three Tiers of Recruitment Agencies

Recruitment agencies (RA), also known as Executive Search Firms, exist in the market for the sole purpose of searching for and placing qualified candidates for positions that are opened by their clients. This concept sounds ideally good, because it works out to be a win-win-win solution for all parties: the candidates (presumably wanting to get a job), the employers (wanting to fill a position), and these agencies (able to earn commissions through successful placements), if things are so simple in reality. RAs can be helpful, because they may have something to offer you when you seek them out, or they may even surprise you with some opportunities you've never heard of while you're not consciously looking, provided that you've already established contact with them. These are the few good things I'd like to say about them.

Most job seekers, especially those who first got into the job market after graduation, often consider RA as one of their go-to source for job hunting. And they are able to get considerable success through RA, especially for junior (and somewhat exploitative) positions that do not pay as well as their education certs' worth. These RAs are on a basic tier-the ones catering to graduates, junior positions, low salary jobs and tend to work on a mass market approach/recruitment drive.

In RA, there are generally three tiers: namely basic, middle and high. Middle tier, as the name implies, cater to the mid income market. They tend to call themselves executive search firms, but in reality they seldom have the capacity to do executive search. They deal largely with mid level/management positions. High tier primarily deals with real executive search. Executives by this definition mean senior executives- positions in the directors to CEO range. They tend to be more exclusive, low profile, discreet in their search, and their company name usually sounds tastefully simple and classier than something with "staffing solutions" in it. The size of the company does not reflect the tier-level; some of the lowest tier RA company has the largest size.

RA, if anything, has to be treated with extreme caution by job seekers, because they are very capable of damaging the reputation and career profile of the candidates. Yes, you read it correctly, and I'll be talking more about it in a while.

As a general rule, basic and high tiered RA are safer than middle tiered RA. Basic RA increases the chances for new or junior level job seekers to land a job through their mass marketing and recruitment drives, which usually do not have much effect on candidate profile because the expectation is not pegged highly for junior/new candidates. High RA adds to the prestige of the candidate for been singled out for exclusive roles in a company. The problem with mid RA is that they try to achieve high RA success with basic RA mentality, because at the end of the day, they are really basic RA agents tasked to handle the mid-tiered job range. And sadly speaking, job seekers deal with the mid RA the most often in their career life.

Recruitment Agents- Salespeople Dealing with the Intangibles

I had work experience as a recruiter in an RA a long time ago. Recruiter is also known as a recruitment agent. An edgier name is headhunter, but that's about the same kind of nonsense. And yes I worked in a mid-tiered one, the one that aspires towards high tier but with basic tier mentality.

From my experience, I can honestly say that all agents working in RA are in reality: glorified salespeople dealing with intangible products- dealing with unpredictable and fickle-minded units known as "human beings" who can back out/spoil a deal if they choose to do so. The problem with dealing with human is that you add the complexity of a human being (which can be quite nonsensical and annoying) as a factor into the product for a business transaction.

Most products sold to customers are considered sold in most business elsewhere. Not always the case for the RA industry. There's always the risk of the candidates not turning up to sign the contact at the last part of the deal closing, something which can happen quite often in this industry.

On top of that, every sales job involves numbers, which is to hit quota of certain revenue for sales target. Things are increasingly harder for the agents these days, due to the ubiquitous amount of similar competitors, the pickier nature of the candidate pool, the growing unwillingness of companies in wanting to engage with recruitment agencies, and the fact that the outsourced recruitment industry is turning into a sunset industry/dying trade with the advent of many job boards who no longer charge companies to advertise their job listings.

With sites like Indeed.com, a job aggregator which pools listings from every sources, the job market is literally at the disposal of the seekers. And HR department at the employers are no longer petrified of the prospects of receiving a heap of unqualified nonsense resumes thanks to several applicant tracking system software which can do the filtering and qualifications. The heydays of headhunting/recruitment, the last time I recalled, was the late '90s to mid 2000 when these technology was non-existent or at its infancy. Things are vastly different now.

As you see, it is not an easy job, even for salespeople standard. So why do so many people sign up to become a recruitment agent if it's so tough?

Sad to say, even during my time, it's an option for people who ran out of options. Most of my ex-colleagues and even myself were graduates who did not score well enough to land a "normal job" with the appalling values and grades in the college transcripts. The others were professionals between jobs who wanted to try something "different" in the interim (and they sometimes grew into this job after getting successes). Many saw this work as a probable recourse/opportunity with the idea that- it is "sale-sy", which may turn out to be lucrative if they manage to do it well, and that it is "easy", because you don't have to bother with intricate details of "normal job", rather you just need to simply deal with human beings. Some people are maybe better in dealing with human beings, but the reality encompasses more than just mere human relationships, but the nonsense they entail.

So more often than not, you'll find many recruiters (from basic and mid RA) with disposition and mannerism similar to used-car salesmen, but comparatively more amateurish and inept, and usually without the technical know-hows (unlike the used-car salesman who knows his stuff), because they themselves may not have engaged with or got deep enough into the actual industries they are representing.

They only have some vague idea of the industries by frequent associations with certain keywords. And they will match the resumes with supposedly workable keywords and spam the hell out to every prospective client whose job descriptors vaguely match those terms.

The modus operandi of the RA agent are rather straight forward, which is to do as much as possible: by securing more clients, finding more candidates for these clients, in view of increasing the chances of placements, and hence fulfilling their KPIs, to minimize the risk of getting sacked for poor performances, and most importantly, to earn commission payouts from successful project closure. Problem can arise when they use many candidates to increase their hit rate, they are also likewise increasing the competition and decreasing the chances of the candidates of securing the jobs.

To all salespeople, everything is a numbers game, and the recruiters will treat candidates not with the best interest, but on how likely the candidates can help them achieve the numbers. Since the commissions and the prestige of closing an expensive candidate (one with high salary) is higher in the mid RA firms, they'd rather work on such people than qualified candidates with lower salary. It's quite common to be left in the cold by these RA agents once they decide that there's not much left to milk from the candidates.

And yet they want your resumes badly, especially if they've not heard of you, because they need to play out the gamble that perhaps you'll eventually be that one prospective lead/unit to close the deal. If you're not that golden ticket for their high commission success, they'll chuck your resume into the "pool of random success", where you'll be sold off to the next highest bidder, so long that your profile can add more digits into their KPIs, than a waste of time (which is ultimately consigned to the Trash bin on their desktop).

Danger of Recruitment Agencies

Any job seekers in the midst of their career (either currently employed or not) should be careful with giving resume to the RA, especially the middle-tiered ones. This is an important forewarning, period.

As I mentioned earlier, the RA can potentially damage your career reputation and profile in the industry. I've also mentioned before that basic and high-tiered RA are comparatively safer than mid RA, which is a chimera with high RA expectations (getting the most payout with expensive project), but with basic RA competency (amateurs without the finesse of seasoned executive search specialists).

Sometimes, the RA can even be an impediment to your job search. It might even be better for you to do without them. I'll list down all the points here to illustrate the case.

1. **Employers are not too keen to use recruitment agencies**- The reason why RA can survive and thrive is due to paying clients. The clients are employers who need the expertise of industry experts to help them seek out suitable candidates to the positions that they open, have no resources to filter or source out "qualified candidates" from their job listings (usually when jobs are listed, all kind of funny resumes come through), or have no satisfactory platform to list their

jobs. From the late '90s to the mid 2000s, there are more RA sought out because job boards charge unreasonable amount of money for job listings and they tend to attract all kinds of unqualified candidates, and classified ads on newspapers are phasing out.

Fast forward to 2020, every job board is now offering job listings free-of-charge to every organization/employer who choose to advertise their positions because the market has gotten very competitive.

There are specialized job sites like LinkedIn and Glassdoor, and there are the job aggregators like Indeed.com, or even recently Google Jobs- which consolidate job listings from different sites and show them throughout the internet. While these job boards may sometimes open up the floodgate to a mass of unqualified candidates to jam up the emails of HR managers, there are increasingly novel applicant tracking solutions which can filter out undesirable candidates.

Unless the clients have already established a special relationship with the RA (which will thus award the RA exclusivity as well as advanced/fixed payment to work on a retained search model), chances are they will not be too keen to even have any dealings with RA. RAs tend to charge a significant amount of fees, which is usually based off a portion of the successfully placed candidate's first year salary (averaging at 30%). Every business, big or small would try their best to cut down on expenses. Why would a company pay money to some agents, when they could find other mean to fulfill the same task? Because of that, most clients prefer to work on their own talent search, or on a non-exclusive basis with the RA, sometimes rather dishonestly so.

Having worked in the RA industry, I had even seen large corporations rescinding on and dishonoring contracts with small to mid-sized RAs, especially the boutique ones. They could disregard improperly formalized contracts, withhold payment, turn around and put fault on the RA firms and even feign disinterest with submitted candidates, only to seek them out after the deal is off with the RA. And sometimes, the projects that are offered to the RA are not even real positions to begin with, but merely a way to fish for market information, or to KIV prospective future candidates (after the RA contracts expire).

The danger that the prospective candidate is likely to face is that the employer who is working through the RA may not even be too keen to finalize the deal, or may merely be using them to study the market. The poor candidate may even be tarred with the same brush with the RA if the latter has a bad reputation. All these result in wasted time and misery for the job seekers.

2. **Recruitment agencies decrease your market value-** That's right, the RA can make your profile undesirable. How do they do so? By several means.

Firstly, they will not just use your profile (gathered through the resume) only for that one job which you applied to. Do not believe in their bullshit promises, they'd sell you out in a moment's notice. They will use your profile to pair with any potential projects that matches some keywords, sometimes not relevantly so because they are not good with detailed nuancing in the industries- they are not industry experts to say the least.

They will likely try to spam your profile to as many employers as possible, to try to increase their rate of success, but at the expense of your market value. If they are somewhat decent, they will at least call you up about such new opportunity and seek your permission to do so, but the problem (and the norm) is that they will usually do it the other way- pair your profile up first, and only contact you if there's some interest from the client- this is a more expedient way in the book of the RAs.

Secondly, if you've worked with more than one RAs, your risk increases exponentially. Imagine you're an employer, and through the several RAs that you are working with, you're shown the same profile over again. You'd be inclined to think less favorably of this candidate because you've probably seen it before, and automatically think he/she is desperate because no one wants him/her. The value of the profile is automatically reduced.

Thirdly, many RA agents are not diligently following the industry practices of "blinding the resume" these days- this practice means that sensitive information like name, workplaces are removed in place for general descriptors to protect the privacy and interest of the candidate.

These practices are however quite troublesome, and since RA agents are working on expediency, to score as many deals in the quickest way possible, they'll gladly submit the whole bloody resume to the clients! And they sometimes feel like this is one solid way to foster trust with the clients by giving information upfront to them who may not like the notion of been given some vague templates to tease their interest. This means that RA agent is highly likely to blow the cover of the candidate, and which will in turn work out negatively if the clients are already disinterested in certain profiles- they'll now know who the bugger is and possibly put this person in blacklist or even talk about this person to others within the industry.

Lastly and most dangerously, if your profile is not successfully placed with the client, your resume will be deposited into the common database for other agents within the company, accessible and free for all. You see, all resumes are sort of like a commodity within the

RA circles. But they can be rendered as junk if they are not treated well. Usually agents like to keep exclusive or exceptional resumes and candidates to themselves but they will have no qualm throwing out the "trash" into the "commons pool" (they usually can't discern the real quality of a candidate, but based it off on the success of either ability to get closed, or eliciting interest from clients). As a result, the unfortunate candidates can be consigned as a spare and easy junk in reserve for random draw, used by newcomers to hone their skills, and abused by other agents who may not know better to represent their interest properly.

3. **Recruitment agencies do phantom job baiting**- I've covered this before, but I'd like to repeat again. RA regularly do deceitful things like phantom job baiting through regular job postings, and even going as far as sharing such scams directly to the candidates. Phantom jobs are non-existent jobs that are made solely for the purpose of getting candidates to send in the resumes when applying.

They usually do this for the purpose of collecting as many resumes as possible to build up their database, so they have an easier time when they finally deal with their clients next time. Or they can reverse sell the profiles to the customers, whichever strategy they choose to employ. If you see job adverts, especially one that is posted and reposted by the same RA on different job boards, there's a good chance that it's one of those fake, phantom job postings. The thing about

RA listing is that they have the advantage of maintaining confidentiality on behalf of their clients, which thus allow them to get away with perpetuating the misdemeanor.

4. **Recruitment agencies increase your competition-** If the RA can over-represent your profile, there's no stopping them from doing the same with other profiles too. The problem with them is that they see a candidate as nothing more than another digit to enable their chances of winning the deal, and since sales is all about the numbers game, they will spam the hell out of every possibility to do so (pushing resumes to every clients). The problem is that the reality of the RA market is tougher than these mindless tricks, due to overwhelming competitions. The agent can do half a year of hard work without closing any deals (that's the maximum period I've seen for unsuccessful agents that lasted that long, before they were asked to go).

The RA firm is bound to have a tough time with competitions, who happen to be the other RA firms. Chances are, if the employer finds one RA firm to do the job, they will try out with at least another two. And that's not even counting the possibility that they could have already listed the job on several popular job boards, including their own website. So let's say that there are at least five sources where the employer will get the candidates. Knowing that it is likely the case, unless you're an exceptionally strong candidate (in which you case you're better off writing directly to the job poster), you know the odds are strongly against you.

Sometimes things can make a difference if the RA is working on exclusivity with the client (which is a special arrangement usually on a retainer model, but that's rarer, and more so for high tiered RA). The problem is that even when the agent told you so, or genuinely believed that is the case, there's no stopping any client from giving false promises, or secretly working with another channel. If things are by default not exclusive, you can be sure that the position the agent excitedly shared with you have already been echoed within the week by several agents in other firms to other people.

Also, when the RA agents tell you that they are representing your profile, it doesn't mean that you are therefore the one and only apple in the eye of the recruiter. They are simply not obliged to do so. Almost hundred-percently, the recruiter will gather at least 2 more profiles to submit together to the clients. The industry practice is about 3-5 profiles for consideration. When you start doing your multiplication from all possible sources, you'll soon realize that you are up against many candidates, and your odds of securing the position may be reduced drastically.

5. **Recruitment agencies can misrepresent the candidates**- Let's ponder this. Who are those people working to represent you? I've mentioned before that a large number of agents are people who either cannot

enter or make it well in the professional industry. These people who are tasked to handle one specialized sector thus may not be well versed enough on specific requirements and nuance of what the employers demand. I've seen countless times agents misrepresenting the candidates, or putting them through wrong job fits.

Usually things are put to a stop before the damage gets any further, if the candidates are discerning, knowledgeable or quick enough to point out to the agent. The damage however is more severe when the agent, having no actual knowledge of the job requirement, give false or misinformation to the candidates and lead them on.

Many agents become more experienced, not because they understand the professional industry they are representing well enough, but learn them largely through keyword associations or through conversations with many clients. And still, they may not get the actual picture at all. Misrepresentation may not be a problem for more general or easier to understood roles, but may turn out to be critical in more technical-based industries.

6. **Recruitment agencies do not have the best interest of candidates**- Often time, RA do not employ a growth mindset on behalf of their candidates. Why would they need to do so, if the candidates are merely some products for them to achieve their goals? Unless they

are specifically told or instructed to do so, they have a tendency to be rather astoundingly stupid in their hunt for candidates and commit the mistake of providing lateral offers, which may turn off potential prospects.

I've mentioned that keywords play a very important role in the operations of the agents in RA, and that extends to the keywords pertaining to the titles as well. To illustrate this case, if the client wants to look for a product manager, they will only start hunting for candidates with the "product manager" keyword in their title. They are usually not interested in helping out the well qualified junior product person who is fully capable of becoming a product manager, but will only stick to this lateral/literal suggestion because they can't do lateral thinking.

The agent is also fully capable of foisting positions onto candidates who are simply not interested, especially if the candidates do not make it in first offered roles, but they quite often do it at the outset. The more unscrupulous agents may take advantage of more "vulnerable" candidates by suggesting that the candidates are simply not good enough and this is the only viable option for them.

7. **Recruitment agencies tend to have poor communications and follow-ups**- Anyone who have dealt with any RAs in their life can attest to the poor communications and follow-ups, especially if he/she did not make it through the rounds. When the RA

identifies a potential candidate, there will be a certain amount of effort to keep things amicable or at least civilly decent. Once the client expresses some interest with the candidate, or wants to proceed with interviews, the RA agent will raise several bars in the friendliness quotient and turn out quite attentive to communications with the candidates.

Just wait until the candidate is dropped out either prematurely or eventually by the client, and you'll witness how fast the agent turn from extreme enthusiasm and friendliness to utter dismissal and indifference. Only rarely are these "professionals" motivated enough to properly follow-up with the candidates, most of the time, they opted to cut off all communications with the failed candidate- not replying emails and messages, or picking up calls; almost poofed out instantly from the candidate's circle, until when the next opportunity comes along that will somehow be helped by the relevance to the candidate's profile, and then we'll see this feigned civility return again. And not only "failed" candidates are prone to be left in the lurch by the RA; clients who do not have successes (not having deals closed and money paid out to RA) for extended period of time with the RA are also treated similarly. And even if there are some successes in the relationship, for both the candidates or clients, RA are notoriously noted for general lack of feedback and poor communications to follow-up for post-sales support, especially after the deal is closed and money paid out.

The Merits and Methods of Direct Application

As I've mentioned before, most employers/companies prefer not to deal with recruitment agencies nor pay them unless absolutely necessary. Surely, it then makes perfect sense for the job seeker to contact the organizations directly, circumventing the troublesome middlemen and getting the resume to the people that counts, and thereby increasing the likelihood of securing a position from the direct source.

I am not asking the readers to therefore cease working with recruitment agents, but rather, to consider direct application as the first priority to increase the chances of success over the use of the agents. Sure, there are companies out there who will only want to work exclusively through their recruitment partners, but those are usually in the minority. If you want to use recruitment agents when there are no direct opportunities to get to, that is perfectly fine, but do not waste your time going through middlemen to get to opportunities that are readily available for direct application.

Often, the easiest way is to go directly to the company's website and look for job openings. Quite frequently, job openings on the company's websites may not even appear or get delayed appearance on the job boards, so you'll definitely get "treasure hunter/early bird advantage" when you do direct applications through here, because most other candidates might have missed them (because they always hang out at the job boards). Once you're done with finding out all the direct openings from the different companies that you're interested in, then go to the job boards next for your job searches.

On the job boards, always look out for postings that are made by the original hirers- the companies or organizations. The postings will usually link to the original company site when you click on something like "apply to company". Otherwise, the postings may link directly to the email address of the person in charge in the company through inmails. These are more straight-forward cases of direct application on job boards.

The less straight-forward approach to direct applications on job boards is to look at the posts made by the recruitment agents. Yes, the same bunch whom I've frequently talked about in the book. Rarely will RA mention the identity of the company, but you can make your inference.

The job descriptors in the posts, whether from the clients they're working on, or copied elsewhere for the purpose of phantom job baiting, are often key indicators to actual opportunities that may appear elsewhere. The resourceful job hunter can copy the entire descriptor, or specific keywords to paste into the search engines to try to find the original sources. Chances are, with some work, you'd be able to find the company and if the positions are still available, to directly apply to them.

From what I observe, a direct application to a role which RA had already been concurrently used for is usually received more favorably by the hirer, because it makes them feel like they've gotten a lucky break when this candidate can be successfully placed, and give them the excuse to drop the RA. Anything that brings about more cost savings for the organization, as well as making the whole engagement process more seamless and less messy without the third party is always welcome.

Technology Can Be An Opportunity Killer

Previously, I encouraged all readers to apply directly when possible: to send in the applications and see how it goes. That is the fundamental in job hunting and ideally there should not be anything wrong with it. But, I was largely arguing for the case of using the direct application in favor of the use of agency, based on the very merit of circumventing the use of middlemen. Let's say that the direct source is reached, and the resume goes over to the other side by now, do you think you will readily hear from them next?

Chances are that you, like everyone else, has probably sent countless applications before, and hardly hear from anyone. Yes, there will be some replies that might come every once in a blue moon, but the norm of job application these days seem to be about sending a ton of resumes to every available opportunities and play the disappointing waiting game. Sending resumes over the internet seem to be such an easy task compared to the old=school paper and mail job applications; everyone can get something over within 15 minutes.

The advent of such technology should be improving the job search situation, and everyone should be readily receiving more opportunities. But that's not the case.

Imagine this- if you can do that resume sending in a matter of minutes, so can anyone with a computer or a mobile phone these days. Just upload and press submit. The problem lies in the receiving end. The person-in-charge who are supposed to receive, read and qualify the resumes is now facing a scary influx of applications flooding the mailbox, thanks to technology.

Do you think that anybody would be able to sit through this endless nightmare? Chances are most of the resumes will not be properly read, or quickly skimmed through for the headlines. If the company have some software to do the filtering, it is also not to the candidates' advantage because they may have exercised unfair algorithmic bias.

If a resume doesn't pique the interest of the one reading it or worst still, simply ignored, even the most qualified person may not be counted for the job, a sad reality which I've discussed about earlier in the book.

Knowing how HR practices are like, they do frequently ignore whole stack of what is considered an eyesore of resumes and instead opt to ask around people they know for candidates. When that happens, hundreds of people had just wasted their time on a fruitless opportunity. And since this kind of thing happened all the time, countless job seekers may have just been wasting a whole lot of their time in the futile quest of applying for jobs.

Leveraging on Employees in The Target Company

Despite the strange irony that technology is actually impeding the chances of helping a person get selected for a job, you should still try to use it for job applications, just more wisely than the other candidates. There's no stopping you going direct and sending resumes in and hey, you might even hear back from those guys after some wait, but if you sense something unusual, like nary a reply despite the fact that you are strongly qualified for a certain position, you might want to get creative and start using technology for all its worth, just not sticking to the same application fest on the job boards, but rather with sites like LinkedIn for example.

Before we get there, we must understand that there are certain limitations and reality concerning and affecting the HR. Firstly, these folks will not know very well your line of work, so they may not know how good you are. Secondly, they may not even have the chance to see your resume, as it could be chucked at a digital corner somewhere in the virtual desert of the unreal. And thirdly, they will usually have separate inboxes that they actually do their daily work on, away from where the bulk of resumes are found.

When you don't hear from them, do not think that by sending an email reminder to the HR will motivate them enough to help you out; they will probably passive aggressively ignore you.

At any point, you should really be thinking about how you can get your resume to the decision maker (HR or not), through a different route that will not put you in jeopardy like the rest of the other unfortunate mass of candidates in the internet folder graveyard.

The solution may actually lie in leveraging the employees in the target company, the internal staffs or colleagues to the hiring person, to act as internal conduit for you to the hiring person. The hiring person is far more likely to respond to an internal staff/colleague than outsiders. Granted that if you already know someone working in the target company, through common associations, or had previous good professional relationships, they might be able to help you out more readily than total strangers.

There are actually many career advisers out there who propose the use of such relationship advocacy as internal referral for job applications. While it can be an effective method, you actually don't know what the person REALLY feels about you. And also, how many of you readers actually know that many people who will readily attest to how good you are, or are able to influence people to help you out in your job search. If you do, you'd have gotten help from them a long time ago, right?

My suggestion is to actually target people who really matters, and who is more neutral towards you, perhaps a total stranger, but who is obligated to act professionally in the organization, like: the decision maker who got the HR to work on those positions, and a middle to slightly more senior person in management. There are different approaches to the two types.

The first type- the decision maker, is usually likely to be your immediate supervisor, or more intimately known as boss, if you ever land up in this role. The HR or the company job posters, being a generalist, is merely listing the jobs on behalf of this person. How do you get to the decision maker? Simply by matching the keywords from the job title, job department and job descriptions to the relevant unit, and then find the relevant head of the unit.

Go to LinkedIn to find out who this person is, and try to ask this person if it is possible to send your resume over for his/her perusal, based on your interest in that specific job. If you find it hard to get connected or correspond with this person over LinkedIn, you may want to try to find his/her work emails by two methods. If the person is connected with you on LinkedIn, you can export profiles and try to find the contact (I mentioned the method to do so earlier in this chapter).

If the person is not connected with you on LinkedIn, you can search for the contact via RocketReach or ZoomInfo. Another person who may also function as the decision maker is a specialized HR person in charge of talent acquisition. This person has the duty to speak to talents, and may not find it easy to reject sincere candidates who need help. Using the same rules, identify this person on LinkedIn if you don't know him or her already, and contact the person.

The second type- a middle or slightly more senior person in management who needs to uphold his/her professional image. Such employees are more conscientious and will not dare refuse help if sincerely approached. Find out such a person in the organization with LinkedIn, and then drop a short note asking for a simple "pass on the message" help. If you don't mind the person to read your resume (although this may not happen), you can write a simple message along the line of something like, "can I trouble you to help me send this document over to Miss ABC, as I encountered some technical difficulties over my outbox?"

The document may be a mail file containing attachment to your resume. If the person did send it over to the HR, the mail will be regarded as coming from a more trusted source within the organization, and secondly it will reach the inbox where mails are properly read, not the one cluttered with all the unread resumes. This email will likely draw the attention of the reader. If you are uncomfortable with asking the guy to handle your resume, you may opt for other simple messages of conveyance like passing the contacts.

Guerrilla Job Hunting Tactics-
The Few Good, Mostly Bad
And the All Ugly

Guerrilla job hunting tactics is all the rage these days, where the concept of guerrilla marketing is applied into the domain of job search by clever authors and coaches. When you take a step back, take a deep breath and look at where such tactics apply, you'll find them usually only serving a small (but important) part of the whole workflow of job search, which is to increase and give visibility of the candidate to the hirer.

By default, most candidates are premised on the reality that they are "invisible" in the job market, due to overwhelming competition, no thanks to technology. Guerrilla job hunting tactics essentially is to apply creative and unusual ways to achieve the purpose of raising visibility for the candidates. The method which I previously mentioned- about using internal staffs to get to the decision makers, can also be considered as some kind of guerrilla tactic, albeit a much more effective one than most of the other guerrilla tactics out there.

Before anyone gets too excited about guerrilla tactics, let's calm down and rationalize if they can really serve any advantage to those who try, and worst, if they can actually backfire. Sure, I began the chapter by asking job seekers to be "different and creative", but to what extent, that's another point to ponder on. There are essentially two main gripes I have with guerrilla tactics that may not be carefully thought out, or done properly:

1. **Devaluation of market value-** Sure, you can orchestrate surprises to spring them on the hirers, but have you thought how much of the fluff will actually see you through to securing jobs at the end? Granted that with most guerrilla tactics, the candidates visibility will almost certainly guarantee to be raised, but is it to good or bad effect? Having the hirer know you doesn't mean that he or she will like you enough to give you the job. Instead, sometimes the hirer will not take such person seriously, or worse still, deliberately make sure that this person does not get the job.

   To understand the psychology of such stunts, try to be a bit more cynical and restraint, and take a look at what else is going on out there in the world: real estate agents' flyers, websites with flashy fonts and popups to "opt-in", YouTube adverts with self-styled gurus in suits and pearly whites. These stuffs are actually thought to be very effective and popular by the marketers. But they almost instantly spell spams and scams to most recipients, with their flashy color and "used-car salesman" sensibility, and most recipients will simply throw away such flyers, boycott such websites, or skip such ads on YouTube than to give them any attention.

   In order to provide better impression and acceptance, people behind the tactics should always be conscious of the nuance, subliminal cues, and most importantly, be able to lead to positive outcomes.

When not done properly, many guerrilla tactics can actually diminish the market value of the candidates, because the latter will then be seen as juvenile, desperate, wheeler-dealer, overzealous or even deceptive if the tactics are too fluffed out, controversial and manipulative.

2. **Inefficiency-** Guerrilla marketing, when it first grew as a popular concept, was intended to be cost effective. However, many guerrilla job hunting tactics are actually pretty costly and inefficient. What are supposed to be simple and clever tactics have turned rather laborious, and which does not always promise results. One of the most classic guerrilla tactic suggestion is to send physical resumes by mail or hand delivery. While I've discussed before the problem with technology, I've also praised some great use of technology. There's no need to go neo-Luddite on emails, because physical copies are not going to help the candidates much.

Sure, we all know that the hirers probably have an inbox full of unread applicants' emails and resumes. The physical method promises that the resume will be guaranteed visibility and attention. I agree with that assumption, but that's only the half-truth. The other half is that after reading the resume, it has a high likelihood to be left in oblivion. Let's be cynical and think through this carefully. I am sure that most of you have probably worked in offices before (in the modern age), and sometimes have to deal with letters. What do you do when you receive them? You might not read them and instead chucked them into the paper pile if you assumed that they were unimportant. Or you might open up and read them and then chuck the content also into that paper pile. That paper pile is almost certainly not touched during the entirety of your stay in the office, because most of your work are done through the computers.

Now, just imagine what will happen if the hirers receive such mails. They may not even dump it into the paper pile, but rather trash them into the bins, because they CANNOT do anything with the resume as all the info is on physical paper, making it difficult for them to copy, paste, edit, send. And mind you, all their works are preferably done on laptop, via digital avenue, because they are already fed up with dealing tons of paper work in human resources. They will most likely get rid of this paper inconvenience than wanting to stay overtime to transfer the information digitally.

There are more severe cases of inefficiency which will simply waste more time and cost for the candidates. These are tactics that encourage the candidate to create and write newsletters or whitepapers to showcase that they are content experts to the potential hirers, involvement with extensive networking and social media schemes, and doing the "work" before and during interviews like writing long cases for their competency, competitive analysis, presentations, and giving the hirers too much benefits upfront without knowing how to subtly negotiate for interests.* These tactics almost certainly will lead to extreme ends of the sunk cost fallacy, which I've touched on earlier before in the chapter, because time and resources could have been used and invested in job hunting in other better ways. (* Exception of this rule: On the other hand, only after you got through the first interview, you can then entice interviewers to open up more interview rounds for you by offering "special" presentations).

Now let's look at the different methods; these are ones that I haven't mention before, and they range from the popular ones that are frequently discussed amongst the guerrilla & fans circles, to the more unusual ones, and you should decide for yourselves if they are worth pursuing.

1. **Coffee Cup Caper**- One of the most famous and talked about, which was purported to have a hit rate of 50-65% of getting interview secured. The job seeker sends three items in a box to the decision maker, namely a resume printed in full color, a cover letter with the words, "can we meet for coffee?", and a paper cup from Starbucks or some other well known coffee establishment. This box is sent by trackable courier and upon receiving delivery notification, the job seeker will then call up and ask the decision maker if he or she has gotten the coffee cup, and then ask again if it is possible to have coffee, and try to fix a date for doing so.

2. **Thank You Note**- The second most famous in that circle, this tactic uses those "thank you" note envelope, with addresses completed and stamped, to deliver the physical resume to the recipient by mail. This is encouraged to be used particularly around festive periods.

3. **Sending Half the Resume**- A deceptive method of sending a very compelling cover letter (with the phone number) in an unsealed envelope to the hirer without the CV, to get them to think that the resume probably fell out, so serving it as a pretext to secure a chance to talk to and sell yourself shamelessly to the hirer when they ring you to ask about that missing part.

4. **Offer Money Back Guarantee**- A rather extreme proposition! The job seeker is basically telling the hirer to treat him or her like an Amazon purchase (that means with possibility of refund), in exchange for getting an opportunity to try out the job.

5. **Social Media Pressure**- This one is more unusual. There's this influencer who detailed her career journey on popular social media platform, and frequently made it a point to let her hirers know her identity (by putting social media links on resume) and that she documented every encounters to all her readers. Misadventures with companies are detailed, and sometimes with social justice shaming like "so I didn't get a job because they see me as a woman?", of course meant as a way to apply social pressure on the

hirers to better accept her, to protect the company's politically correct image.

6. **Moral Obligation**- Getting (and pressuring) religious leaders and fellow believers who might be employees of desired organizations in the secular life, to support and ensure fellow brothers and sisters from the same order in this "do-gooder/God-fearing" network to get the jobs.

Tapping into the Hidden Job Market

Beyond what is apparent and publicly available, there are jobs and opportunities that are not in plain sight or which you're not aware of, and for that you may have to delve deeper.

What you see and know may not constitute the whole reality. On the internet, almost all of the users can only access 5% of what is out there, and that portion constitutes the part known as the "surface web". Beyond that, 95% goes into "deep web" and "dark web" whereby only those with specialized browsers and tools, who looked hard enough, and of certain privilege can venture into.

Likewise, things are similar in the job market. What you see on the job boards or classifieds ads is not the full picture of what is available. The obscure part is known as "the hidden job market" and it constitutes 50% of the totality of the real job market.

The "hidden job market" of course should not be likened to something as dark or sinister as the "deep or dark web", but comparable on the basis of exclusivity and secrecy. To put it in simpler terms, the positions, hires and placements are simply not conspicuously announced or advertised, but only shared either internally, through professional circle, or through personal network and contacts.

Most job seekers who are out on the hunt will likely only use job boards, recruitment agents or apply through company websites, not knowing that there's such a thing as the "hidden job market". Consider this: if you can access this hidden job market, you have more advantage over these job seekers when you can go where the others cannot.

There must be good reason why such opportunities may be deliberately hidden from plain sight, and they are usually because of the sensitive nature of some positions, for example, a replacement position that is to be kept secret from the incumbent and other colleagues, or new positions that will potentially undermine the competitors. And cronyism, and other less than savory way of keeping things in the "family" so as to speak are pretty common too.

But actually one of the most common reason for hidden opportunities is simply due to the fact that they somehow just did not make it to the public domain, because the HR forgot to do so or didn't see the need to, that's all. Therefore, resourceful job seekers shouldn't let up on such opportunities if available.

There are several ways to tap into the "hidden job market". One of the more obvious way is to simply ask someone who is working in that company or industry. They may not mind helping you out if there's handsome referral given by the company. You may already be acquainted with them to enquire about such opportunities. And even if they don't know you, you already know how to get such people, because I shared you a hack that allow you to get their email addresses through LinkedIn. Another obvious way is to be involved in the community that the personnel of these companies are involved in. Exclusive information may be shared within these circles. But actually these two obvious ways may turn out to be the hardest for the average readers here, who may not have the necessary network and contacts for such endeavor.

The third way is perhaps the easiest to achieve, that is if you are of decent intelligence. It is entirely through- research. Get a sense of the company's direction by the activities that are put out. For example, if a company performs a merger & acquisition with another, there's bound to be restructuring happening sooner or later, whereby a significant number of the staffs in the acquired company will be booted, and which you can be sure that opportunity will be created in the midst.

Another example is to look at the financial report. If the company is not doing well, there will certainly be shuffling in "more redundant" departments, for example like marketing. This department will usually get trimmed, or replaced with cheaper leadership, who is likely to get his/her own staffs. Also frequently up the news and press releases, they are excellent indicators of the company's direction. Companies who announce that they are in the process of coming up with a new product will surely need positions to be filled in anticipation for product launch, which is a great opportunity to start writing them to offer your service.

The next few topics are other methods for your consideration.

The Recruitment Agents Stratagem

Recruitment agents are not always all bad. There's only so much an individual know, and the RA agents can sometimes be counted upon as a rather valuable source of information. They may even lead you to some opportunities that are within the "hidden job market". I personally do not like to use them for applications due to their unreliability, but if they are from the higher tier ones, or if they have exclusivity for some opportunities, I wouldn't mind them. In fact, I love to talk to to them, whether I intend to go with them or not, because they are always able to tell me something that I don't know; not because they are industry experts, but because they are frequently engaged in the "hidden job market".

While most employers really don't like to work with them, sometimes they will still inevitably do so because these RA have some advantages. One of the many reasons why some employers inevitably end up with the recruitment agencies is because they've difficulty in finding suitable candidates themselves and want to count on their network. There may also be other reasons like the need for a partner to handle sensitive roles requiring confidentiality (usually replacement roles), or simply as an outsource for the tedious work of filtering and qualifications.

Knowing how RAs are like, they are certainly not the most preferred option for the job seekers. But if you know how to make use of them wisely, you may be able to use them, without you committing anything to them. Indeed, I've used them quite a bit in the past to unravel unadvertised opportunities or opportunities that I haven't come across, without the obligation to commit to them (and that was after my stint in the RA so I knew most of the tricks up their sleeves). And I'll show you how this can be done.

When RAs contact potential candidates, they can do one of two things. They will either keep mum on the identity of the prospective clients until the candidates are almost certainly guaranteed first interview with the client, or they may divulge earlier to maintain the interest of the candidates, and to minimize the likelihood of the candidates losing interest after some progress has been made.

When the RA contacted me, I always requested/demanded them to reveal to me the identity of the client they were working on before we continued our conversations. They were able to reveal identity about 70% of the time, because they wanted to ensure my interest and not waste time.

Usually after learning about the identity of the client, and knowing the job description (they either verbalized or sent a separate email detailing the JD), I expressed disinterest about this role to the RA. Well, that's me, you don't have to do the same. Anyhow, at that point, I was no longer on the list of the RA for this particular role. But with some idea about the client and the role, I was able to go to the company's website, search the career/HR email and wrote them about this role (make sure that this is not one of those top secret roles or it will surely backfire and land both you and the RA in trouble; there are other ways to handle super confidential roles which I'll share with you). And only when they consented, I sent my resume over. I managed to successfully clinch at least one job through this method.

But the other 30% of the RAs were more insistent in maintaining the secrecy of the identity of their client, as perhaps the confidentiality was paramount. What I got them to do, without relenting to give up my resume to them, was to request the title of the role, and the job descriptor of this role on word document for my consideration.

The RAs were smart enough to blank out the name of the hirer, but through a bit of sleuthing, I could still easily track down the company behind the job title and descriptor by noting the use of certain keywords, like the kind of things they do, specific terminology they use (some terms are used exclusively by one or few companies), as well as other indicators (location, region of coverage, reporting structure, product nature, etc).

Through inference, I was able to find out the original hirer, even though there's no such opportunities that are listed anyway. And I would usually be cautious in my dealing with the potential hirer, writing to them to ask for opportunities while purposely showing off my skillsets relevant to that "secret role" for their perusal, instead of blatantly pointing out my interest for that particular "secret" role.

Of course, you don't have to pull such ruses on them, and just go ahead with passing them the resume, but you are doing all this at your own risk. Also, if the RAs can get to the level of handling confidential/exclusive positions, they tend to be more trustworthy and reliable.

Reverse Application

Still no luck despite all the efforts in your job hunting? Maybe you'll like to take matters into your own hands. The "hidden job market" may be there, but sometimes it is created for you by yourself. Confused? Well, then read on.

I had mentioned before that with the advent of technology, you're up against serious competitions; for any jobs that are posted online, there will be influx of applications that went in and chances are, the HR may not be able go through them and properly find qualified candidates. It's not just the amount of time spent in job searching, or the amount of jobs you applied to that will ensure your success; rather it is your resourcefulness. You need to target where it matters, to get the attention of the right people, and beyond that, to unravel hidden opportunities or even create your own opportunities.

Rather than passively wait for opportunities to materialize, you might want to consider to proactively ask for one. I call this the "reverse application", whereby you reverse the process of job hunting by asking for one. It is completely legal and appropriate to write to the relevant authority to ask for opportunities. The opportunities may be something which exist in the "hidden job market" and not publicized, or it may even be created for you, created out of nothing. And if there are no ready opportunities, this gesture may put you in consideration for future opportunities if there are any.

In order to do this, you need to first understand the right kind of target audience. The contact should reach the decision makers, or those that matters. You'd not want the messages to be ignored, or worse still, getting picked up by people not friendly to you. Look at the kind of company you hope to work in. Is it a startup to medium enterprise in size, or is it a multi-national corporation? Do they even have their own human resources employee?

Mind you, not every company have human resources personnel or department. But if they do, you need to understand how these HR folks operate. The HR employees are just like everyone else, who will only work bare minimum necessary to bring in the dough, when specifically instructed to do so. They, especially the more junior HR staffs will not take any initiative or care enough to make a difference for anyone, and will most likely ignore your email or resume if they are not in charge of the recruiting process. While most people have the impression that the HR staffs have the easiest job at work, it's quite the contrary in reality- they have to take care of everybody's shit in the company. The person at the HR department who is posting for the recruitment is usually designated to do so, specifically for a certain sector/department.

So, if you fancy working in a specific role/department in a glamourous MNC, you should remain cautious about writing to the general HR email (that is if you can even find it at all). There's a good chance that it will not be read, but gets automatically forwarded by the mail server to a common folder for someone to pick up (the common folder is usually ignored), or marked as spam or junked.

Instead of spamming the HR in a big company, you should examine the HR departmental structure and hierarchy within the company. Use LinkedIn and check out who is the department head, and/or which HR staff is handling the relevant portfolio, or who is a recruiter. It is especially helpful if that person has a title with words like "Talent Acquisition". You should try to connect with this person via LinkedIn (or if you have their email addresses, even better) with a sincere message/note about wanting to connect. Later in this topic there are details about the steps you need to follow when you make first contacts. If you're ignored, don't worry- that means they are not doing their job properly and you should look elsewhere.

If you couldn't get to the person through LinkedIn and also yielded nothing through web searches, you can always get the person's contact (name, title, email and even phone number sometimes) by using RocketReach and/or ZoomInfo, as last resorts.

Do bear in mind that some of these people in the HR, especially talent acquisition people, are the gatekeepers to opportunities within the company. If you can be nicely acquainted with some, the upside is limitless. If there are no available opportunities at the moment, you can still be considered for the next in the future. Usually people, including those in the HR, can be rather biased. If they like you enough they will consider you over others.

In smaller sized companies, sometimes there's only one person who handles the HR. This person has the the duty to take care of all human resources matter. With that, it is possible to write directly to the HR email address (smaller companies tend to display their HR and/or Job Application email addresses), and chances are it will be read. For those companies without HR (usually startups or small enterprises), even the CEO will read every email that comes in through. If you can find a general purpose email on the website, or the LinkedIn profile of the guy in charge of this company, you should consider writing or connecting directly with this person, because he/she most likely be the decision maker.

After you've identified your target and decided to contact them, you should try to do several things. As a rule of thumb, do not write long messages. Keep it short and simple, but with clear intent. Thank them first for their attention. Write or talk about the skillsets you have, and how you would like to contribute to the specific department via specific role. Highlight the value proposition> how your presence will help the function. Use keywords that will interest them.

Then ask them for availability to discuss about opportunities. Do not ask for work opportunities in the first contact, because if they replied no or ignored your message, that's a deal breaker. You should really aim to have a proper discussion with them. Once they replied, either positively to agreeing to talk to you, or negatively like they have no time/redirect you to some website, or telling you no need to because they do not have anything at the moment, you should always follow-up on wanting to send your resume over for consideration/deposit, provided they've not already asked you to do so. Do not send over any resume if you don't hear any replies at all.

There's no guarantee that they will give you any opportunity eventually, but you should still try to take steps to get acquainted with them. You can slip a reason/excuse in after they accepted your resume, by suggesting that you'd like to thank them by buying them coffee. If they accept, you're on the first step to building a relationship. Most people wouldn't resist such nice gesture, but if they do (they could be really busy), at least you should be comforted to know that you've already planted a seed of positive impression in their head.

The External Professional

Yes, many people are liable to be hell-bent on getting a position in a company, to be gainfully employed, because that's the only source of income they know. But if a person is resourceful enough, he or she can still get paid income by the same company, but without subjecting the self to the whims and fancies of the employers. And if you've no luck in getting a job for a while, maybe that's destiny's idea to get you to work on something far better than a job?

If you have difficulty in securing job opportunities in the market, why don't you proactively create the opportunity for yourself? Take the "Reverse Application" concept I've discussed previously, and then extend that idea further- by offering your service to the company, even if they're not actively looking for help. Make them an offer they cannot refuse. Sure, they may choose to hire you instead (which can be a good thing), but if they are not sure if they want to have a headcount (which can be expensive, like taxes, etc) and yet need something to be done, they may be able to count on you.

If you can get there, you're technically not an employee of the company, but a business partner of sorts, the "external professional". And that also technically make you a businessperson. While you're running the show as a businessperson, you need not subject yourself to business risks/cashflow issues that are associated when you run it all yourself because you're paid by the company.

As an external professional, you also do not need to commit yourself totally to any organization. You just need to do the project properly- yes, the work assignments are treated as projects, and you'll be free from the usual bullshit in employment: the politicking colleagues or the need to pretend to look active infront of your desktop. Usually if you are an external party, you are not even obliged to be in the office unless necessary. You can work from home and do your stuff, that way you want. You can even pick up several projects from other companies at one go if you're up for it.

Most companies, especially smaller ones, or those that are looking into expansion or innovations, are usually quite open to interesting suggestions or services that are offered, provided that they make sense and can help the bottom-line and top-line. Better still if the companies are facing a certain bottleneck that the only right kind of person like yourself can help resolve.

The thing is, most people are naturally averse to such a "scary notion" because they are not familiar with it. Many would first think that they are not qualified enough to pull such a thing. Well, you don't need to have a wealth of experience although it doesn't hurt to have them. You can make do even with just one or two years of having done something in the past. It really depends on how you are selling yourself to the companies. All that matters when you're selling your message is to be the right person to address what the company lacks, while highlighting the "results and successes" of what you had done, and what could be possible for them.

As working adults (presumably), we all probably know the most typical type of external professionals are consultants. The ones that do consulting and work in a consultancy (usually their own), giving expert advice to their clients. When we talk about consulting, we might be inclined to think of those fanciful management consultant types from McKinsey or Bain.

But there are so many independent consultants out there who can eke out a living without having those shiny accolades. And I personally know many independent consultants who existed because they couldn't or didn't want to get the next job as an employee. If you've got advices that you can offer that can help some companies' business, go ahead and be a consultant, that's the most common type of external professionals.

What I'm trying to tell the rest of the readers is that you don't need to be a consultant, or a guru who knows a lot about the industry. You just need to be someone who can do things that the company is not able to. I'll give you some ideas with some examples.

Let's say you're a person who stays in, and had some experience with sales and marketing of medical devices in Timbuktu. Timbuktu may be slated to become the next hottest emerging market. An American medical device company may be thinking of expanding their presence into this part of the world. If you do your homework, you'll know that it's maddeningly expensive and troublesome for a foreign company to set up an office and presence in Timbuktu. As the resourceful guy, you might want to write to this company and tell them that you will be the "outsource partner for sales and marketing" and ask them to consider this arrangement. That's how things begin. Any careful yet skeptical company will weigh out the costs and still consider it cheaper and less risky to pay you fees for your work than to waste a lot more with recruitment drive, paying fixed salary (and hidden costs), and expensive overheads.

Second example: a video game startup who has all the brilliant coders but no artist on board. The rates offered by graphical artists out there can be quite exorbitant but hey, since you've got the talent with graphic design, and you're between jobs, surely it's not a bad idea to write them to propose your help, in return for decent fees lower than those expensive market rates. And since you enjoy drawing and other artistic pursuits, you do not have to stick with just one project, but can pick up multiple projects for you to express your artistic talent, while making good money at the same time. And before you know it, you may turn into the go-to person for all video game arts after you have built a solid portfolio.

The last key benefit of working as external professionals is that it can also be a really good way to cover the gap that may start forming when you're in between jobs. You can use it as the reason to justify the long gap from your last job to the next employer; additionally, it can also be a novel option to try to get income after unsuccessfully applying to jobs, treating it as a special period to do something differently like honing your entrepreneurial skills, or you may want to stick around to let it grow bigger, to be not subjected to the slavery of employment anymore. There's no hard and fast rules and you can start/stop anytime you like.

Covidian Opportunities

"For the gods perceive future things, ordinary people things in the present, but the wise perceive things about to happen." (Philostratus)

Covid-19 has certainly brought about much misery to humanity. The pandemic has destroyed and disrupted many lives and economies, with widespread lockdowns within and between countries bringing air-travel, hospitality, entertainment industries and many private enterprises to their knees, causing massive spikes in unemployment. I am sure all readers can relate to what I am saying.

Of utmost concern for most people is how soon we are going to find ourselves out of this mire. Until the next vaccine is announced, most people will remain uncertain about the future. And even after the next vaccine is effectively in place, most of the world will likely not resemble the old world ever again. Jobseekers, employed or not, who find themselves amid this period will probably realize their prospects dire and limited. There's a great amount of unemployment rising, as people lost their jobs and/or get laid off as industries collapse and companies start to downsize in preparation for the worst to come. With the huge mass of people looking for job, and with many jobs and opportunities dwindling, job hunting is going to be much harder than ever before.

Something is happening in the background. There's plans for The Great Reset, and no, it's not something conjured from conspiracy theorists and tin-foil hatters, but a reality considered as an initiative by The World Economic Forum. This great reset, beginning with the global financial systems reshuffling and the ongoing healthcare crisis, will see the creation of new rules of governance and engagement, a paradigm shift to a digital age, and perhaps the greatest gift to all globalists, the implementation of the new world order.

Whether you're in for it or against it, the new world order is going to come, and in itself presents great opportunities for the jobseekers. In crisis looms opportunity; we've seen how much online and health-related businesses are booming amid the pandemic. But my vision of the world going forward is actually quite the contrary of what the new world order intends- the globalization of the past 200 years will actually become increasingly deglobalized from 2020, and we will see countries and people breaking up the global network with the creation of self-sufficient silos for- agriculture (food), self-wealth (unlinked to banks), and stability (security) as a way of life in the near future.

Let's first look at some of the current opportunities that have been going on for a while since the Coronavirus crisis. There are increased manufacturing of PPE protective gears and facemasks. There are the mass recruitment drives to deal with patient sample collection, lab testing, patient care. And pharmaceutical companies are researching on, running clinical trials, and racing to come up with the most effective vaccines. Many people were hired for the above purposes.

On the other hand, due to the lockdowns and social distancing, there are many online-based businesses that are also doing particularly well in this time period, because people turn to phone apps and the internet for most of their shopping and services needs instead of going to the traditional brick and mortar shops, like Uber Eats for food delivery and Zoom for teleconferences. Businesses who did not effectively make it in time to transit online are immensely crushed, but those with significant online presence are doing rather well.

On the negative side, most of the jobs pertaining to these industries are largely catering to junior, temporary job workers, as well as unskilled/workers in career transitions. The employers used to pay handsome sum in the beginning of the pandemic, due to the risk of such work (and presuming that it will not last that long), but when the pandemic continues and more people are getting jobless, they're now paying measly sums, and will usually sign up people for "internship" which is just a clever way of cost cutting.

In order to make sense of what is to come, it is important to get a sense of a post-Covid scenario. I have come up with a list, a look at what is happening in reality now, and what is likely to come. This is of course just my personal opinion.

1. **Company Restructuring**- Many big companies (those not destroyed by the pandemic) are making use of the Covid-19 crisis as a pretext to go lean. For the past decade or so since 2008, there's an increase in many expensive senior management and executives forming at the top of organizations, making company hierarchy

"unstable" and costly. 2020 is a prime opportunity to plan for such grand purge. And when such things happen, entire departments can vanish along with their leaders.

Incidentally, this period sees the largest increase in "phantom jobs" on job boards. I daresay that there's almost 80% of them infiltrating the market now. These positions are meant as massive resume/data collection drive, and there are actually very low fill-rates for these jobs at the moment, because most of the headcounts are actually frozen. The collection of the resumes is anticipated for the resumption of hiring, when the pandemic is under reasonable control. That will kick in the restructuring process, with the great purge, and the extensive hiring.

My advice to professionals looking for job opportunities: while you may not be getting news/positive outcome right now, fret not, because your skillsets are irreplaceable by graduates coming out from college, as well as professionals from other industries, and you will find yourselves gainfully employed again, once the situation is under control, perhaps in a better place than you had.

On the other hand, even when situation is not really improving in the near future, at some point it would have become a norm and companies will have to accept and adjust into this reality, and to commence the hiring process if they decide to remain competitive in the market, although they will certainly work on leaner operations, and the employees may be tasked to be multi-functional. It's always a good idea to send your resumes to the dream Big 4s you hope to work for right now, and it's normal to not hear back from them for now; you never know if you'll be placed in their lists of considerations.

2. **The Next Baby Boom**- Actually much of healthcare are not doing well right now, if you dig deep enough. It's only those healthcare companies with capacity to get into infectious disease and molecular testing for Covid-19. Those healthcare companies who manage to jump onto the bandwagon register huge growths that cover up the severe deficit in their other businesses. One of the greatest Covid-19 victim within the healthcare industry is the Reproductive Health business. Most people are simply not in the mood to have kids in times of crises.

This market crashes by almost 80% in most parts of the world. But imagine what will happen when the pandemic is under control? There will be a new wave of increased pregnancies. And for that, the demand for such pregnancy tests, prenatal/postnatal care, and baby products will increase, and thus, the corresponding job opportunities. If you've experiences in these area, you may want to position yourselves to get onboard once it starts.

3. **Jobs in the New Digital World**- I think the digital age is coming very soon. The main narrative of the Great Reset is a new financial system. All industries that exist in support for the implementation of such a system will even greatly surpass healthcare. The whole Covid-19 tests and medicine part will taper off at some point, but industries tied to the Great Reset will only get bigger and bigger.

The post-Covid world will probably see the development of the cashless society with interoperability between connected global entities, starting with rolling out cash-to-cashless matrix, digital identities for the populace (which is concurrently going to happen with the pandemic resolution), integrating voice and contactless payments with instant payment infrastructure seamlessly, ensuring of data protection and transparency, creation of payment continuity plan and implementation of awareness programs. Cyber security and fraud forecasters will be in demand, and there will be facilitators between traditional financial institutions and fintech start-ups to advance innovation, and study payment experiences. Those with finance, banking, IT, system security, cryptocurrency, technology, sales and marketing background will probably find themselves valued and sought after in this new digital age.

And we've not even talked about the other aspects of digitalization yet. In my opinion, while there will be increased online transactions for all kinds of goods and services for precisely the opposite of globalization: silo communications via teleconferencing, and although global travel will likely resume in the post-Covid world, it will not be significantly reduced. Other tech-based industries where I see potential growths are in **agriculture** (yes the most important), **renewable energy**, artificial intelligence, space, cryptocurrency, virtual reality, virtual teaching/events, telemedicine, bionics, modular gadgets and quantum computing. The world will be more fragmented and insular as a result, yet ironically connected and wired online.

On the other end of the spectrum, people will become more interested in taking care of health in the holistic manner, which encompasses not just physical health, but mental health and even spiritual health. There will be more demands for alternative lifestyle and the arts.

4. **Bridging Now to the Future**- There will be many outsource operations, and demand for flexible, and modular expertise. Companies would increasingly consider leaner outfit and take advantage of modular capabilities for certain functions. The valued employee of the Covidian age are those who can be resourceful and self-sufficient, and have the capability for specific skillsets and yet wear multiple hats. The employees can also expect more flexible working environment, and remote operations (work-from-home), where the job permits, as companies are trimming operations, and even closing down whole offices as cost-cutting measures to do away with the overheads. The work-

from-home thing will likely become the norm even into the future, as companies realize that there's actually some cost-benefits to it (they were apprehensive in the past until it happened for them to find out its benefits). Those who are not keen to travel in the past may now be able to take up a regional role without the need to travel. Business travels in many countries may not totally resume or get easier for a long time, which gives the excuse for the employee to do regional work via the computer at the comfort of home.

Likewise, temporary jobs are the norms these days and are comparatively easier to get into than permanent positions, as most companies are unsure about what is to come. In order to play safe, they will offer short term contracts, and/or part time for cost cutting. Some jobseekers prefer temporary positions, but for those in need for permanent positions, since they are so hard to find these days, it is probably more prudent to take up the temp jobs first, because later on, perhaps near the end of contract, the Covid situation may improve and/or the employers may value the skillsets, warranting the possibility of re-negotiation for a permanent position.

While no one can tell when you'll be able to get a job at the present, it doesn't hurt to fill up your time by educating yourself and learning new skills, in preparation for the new opportunities and to thrive in the post-Covid world, which is going to be a new world you never knew, until now.

3. The Interview

Congratulations to those who manage to clinch interviews. If you get this far into the job search, the chances of securing a job opportunity would have increased tremendously. It is not easy to find good opportunity, to get the resume to the right person, and have it selected for consideration. You'd have passed through the first gate by the admittance of the gatekeepers, but there are still some hurdles you need to get around. Admittedly, this part is what makes the job search process stressful for most applicants.

Interviews, whether done through face-to-face meetings or over phone/teleconferences, bring the candidates to meet with the hirers and stakeholders, and in a way it is a test of wits, speech and luck. At this critical moment, and having come this far, all candidates hope not to fail this test. Yet there are many people who find this a difficult juncture, feeling jittery about unknown challenges and difficult questions that are posed by the interviewers. And even when you passed the first round, there might be several more rounds to go through.

While the candidates would find themselves faced with less competitions compared to earlier processes of application, the competitions are still there, though more rigorously considered, and it is especially disheartening to make it far into the selection, only to fail at the last round of the interview.

But a little confidence and knowledge goes a long way. Yes, do what is necessary- prepare to regulate your emotions, stay positive, be friendly and polite, and dress appropriately; these things I'll not go through because they are easily understood.

Instead, I will share with my readers effective and logical ways to increase your chances in these critical and determinative stages, by showing you the underlying psychology behind interviews, the subtle art of increasing your chances and decreasing the odds, and other strategies, most of them not mentioned elsewhere yet representing much of the reality during interviews. The things I share should increase your confidence and knowledge, because you are privy to things that are not mentioned or understood by most people, career coaches included.

The Best Interview May Not Guarantee a Job

Have you ever wondered why you're still not hired for the job even though the interview went exceptionally well? There were great camaraderie and approvals during the meetups, and you actually managed to answer all questions in a clever way, had all your positive points covered, and met all the criteria for this job. When you checked back, you found out that they actually settled for this ex-colleague of yours, who wasn't impressive as a person, was a whole lot inept about the skillsets, and even had a bit of a stammering problem. On the other hand, have you also had experience before when you still manage to clinch a job deal despite screwing up the interview, where questions were not properly answered? Well, this is a slice of the reality in the job market, in the same vein as why the most qualified will not get the job.

I had worked as a recruiter as well as an employer before so I had been through a good amount of the hiring and interview processes, and trust me, they are nothing like what many career coaches talked about. It really boils down to perspectives; the career coaches could have more experiences themselves as candidates attending interviews, or maybe as recruitment agents facilitating interviews, but seldom with the experience in decision making. From the decision makers' point of view, many of the candidates who perform the best in interviews do not get the job eventually. I'll tell you why.

There are too many career coaches who focus on the form, rather than the substance of the interview and encourage the interviewees to try to impress as much as possible. But in my opinion, I think it's a dangerous move because there's a high chance of backfiring which thus deviate much from intended outcome. I think interviews should not be considered as the time for the candidates to impress the hirers; rather **it should be the time for the candidates to remove doubts from the hirers**. Interviews are held to get the hirers to find out more about the candidates, so they can be more certain about the candidates' supposed experiences as stated in the resumes. Sometimes an interview that is done too well, or too impressive will instead, cast doubts to the hirers.

Interviews are certainly important, but they only play a part in the hiring process. When several interviews are performed, the findings are gathered, and will need to be rigorously considered, not just by the decision maker, but generally also in consensus, usually with the boss of the decision maker, if not, with the rest of the team. During my time as a decision maker, I had candidate whom I like who did not make the cut, due to disapproval by the team and/or my superior. Likewise, I also had candidates who I immensely disliked getting approval from the same people.

Often, the candidate may get rejected at the outset during the first interview without even going through the consensual approval. There are several reasons behind this:

1. **Prejudice and Bias**- There are just some people who simply don't like the way you look, the way you dress, how you behave or where you come from. I had often seen very qualified candidates getting turned down by hirers over the simple reason of not liking the face or the vibe that the person gave off. Prejudice and bias are beyond our control, but at least we can try to act as civilly and positively possible during an interview to try to minimize any possibility of inducing dislike. And it will also certainly help somewhat if you can try to learn about the hirers beforehand and customize your interview persona accordingly to the different nature/type of the hirers.

2. **Culture Fit**- Despite all the greatness of the candidate, if he or she is not the right cultural fit, then it will also greatly affect his/her chances of securing the job. The best example is a dynamic, go-getter, sharp smooth-talker type- if this person is applying for a techie role, he or she will most definitely get rejected, because the hirer is uncomfortable to have this type in their rather more insipid techie dullsville.

3. **Budget**- In smaller business outfits, sometimes they may not be able to fulfill the hiring of certain candidates due to budget limitation. The candidate may be very suitable in all aspects, but commanding a last drawn salary, and asking for a salary that are way above the limits of the headcount budget. For that reason, such overpaid candidates may be dropped due to budgetary

constraints, in place for cheaper alternatives who may not even do the job half as well.

4. **Threat**- Yes, hirers and decision makers can get threatened by the candidates who are too good, particularly if they also have bosses to report to. The candidates are supposed to be their prospective subordinates, which means that they should be good enough for the role, but not stand a chance to potentially replace the person. Candidates who display exceptional talent, command exceptional presence during interviews, or who have exceptional criteria beyond the job role, will most likely stir up insecurity within the decision makers, especially if the latter are middle management salarymen.

The take home message here, once again, is to not be too overtly focused on impressing the interviewers, since it will likely transgress on some of the points above, particularly point 1 and 4. Your key to securing the job is to make use of the interview to remove all doubts that the hirers or key decision makers have about you, and get them comfortable enough to invite you into the job. Do not worry too much about those possible transgressions; there are many ways to get around the interview process to increase your chances of success if you can remain mindful. You can begin by taking a more nuanced approach, and customize your persona for each interview you are having. Remember, adaptability is the key, and it's applied differently to different people. But before we get into the different personas you should consider adopting, let's first look into the psychology of the interviewer.

Psychology of the Interviewer

There are essentially two types of interviewers. One type are the Facilitators, who are typically people from the HR tasked by decision makers to recruit, talent scout, or review the applicants. They usually do not know much about any job function, save for the job descriptors or some of the key phrases they frequently come across from the different job functions.

When they request for interview, they are either vetting the candidates in a preliminary round from selected profile, before passing successful candidates to subsequent decision makers, or they are facilitating the team to interview this person together.

The second type are the Stakeholders. Now, the Stakeholders are primarily the decision makers, but can also encompass other team members. Decision makers as Stakeholders will most likely end up as the direct supervisor of the successful candidate, and they are the ones who know the job functions well, and will ask the most questions.

The involvement of other Stakeholders like the team members are sometimes used in some interviews as a way to suss out more from the interviewee, as well as to get a sense of how the rest of the team feels about this person.

Generally, what the Facilitators are looking out for are the few things below:

1. **Veracity of the Information**- They will do a first level glance across all the different experiences and education stated, and then run through with the candidate to see if there is any consistency or lack thereof, between what is written in the resume and what is mentioned during the interview.

2. **Summary Building and Notes Taking**- Before they let the candidate through to the next round, they will need to build a summary case for the decision makers. Seldom do they make decisions in their own round, like rejecting the candidate thereafter and not put up the summary case to the decision makers, unless there are good and strong reasons for doing so (e.g. wrong job fits or horrible attitudes from the candidates). In order to build up the summary, the Facilitators will attempt to get a sense of why the candidate leave the last role, what motivated him or her to join this company, and the key highlights between the different job experiences.

3. **General Sense of the Attitude**- This is very important. While the HR people tend to get bureaucratic after a while, there's one aspect they never let up, and that is with human behavior and interpersonal dynamics. Things we thought of as mere superfluous platitude are taken seriously in the HR business, because they are supposed to be in-charge of all affairs human. They often use the interviews as a chance to practice (and

showcase) their human reading skills, and would gladly report about their observations, be it the behavior, attitude and even subtle cues of the body language as part of the summary report.

4. **Potential Problem with Hire**- Last but not least, the Facilitators have to make sure that this person is hirable. Several common considerations are about the person's notice period, if the person is under non-competition clauses, whether there's any need to apply for work visas, or if the person's expectations can be met.

For the Stakeholders, they are usually more critical about the interview, because they will be responsible for the consequences and outcome of making the decision to hire and have this candidate onboard, with lasting effects that can affect the whole department. While the HR is more casual with the profiles unless something piqued their interest, the Stakeholders on the other hand will tend to want to know more about the candidates they are interviewing. If they have time available at hand, they may even snoop on the candidates, to try to find out the secret social life through social media like Facebook (hence it always helps for any job seekers to clean up their social profiles prior to applying for jobs).

Here are some of the things that go through in their heads during the interview processes:

1. **The Hope to Get the Right One**- Interview can be a time-consuming and tedious process. In order to get

closure on one headcount, they have to commit several one-hours to several candidates, which tend to steal away their valuable time, particularly when they come from middle to senior management. Therefore, the wishful thinking of any Stakeholders, prior to any interview, is to hope to get and close the right candidate at this one. Things tend to get more desperate if they still haven't found the right candidate after a long period of time. **In this sense, sometimes late applicants to a job posting may find themselves getting increased successes than the early applicants**.

2. **Ability to Solve Problems and Not Cause Problems-** Jobs are created precisely to solve problems. The most eligible candidates are the ones who are able to solve current and future work problems, as well as not to bring any problems to the boss, team and organization. The first indicator of course are the job experiences and skillsets. Appropriate experiences should give the person the ability to handle challenges and resolve problems. The second indicator is the ability to then function in the team, if there is any. The prospective candidate needs to be able to immerse successfully into the company/department culture without complaints, and be able to work with one another effectively. The third indicator is about the liability of threat. Will the introduction of this person upset the status quo? Will this person overtake and threaten the boss's position in the company one day?

3. **Value and Affordability**- In conjunction with the HR, the Stakeholders must decide whether this prospective candidate will therefore add value to their department or organization, or to meet the budgetary limits that are set for them to utilize. Candidates who are more liable to get employed usually offer the best cost-benefits. All job seekers should also be conscious of one thing: the value you offer and propose should be something of benefit to the Stakeholders, and not strong enough to threaten their livelihood and cause insecurity.

4. **Opportunity to Gather Info**- Often time, the Stakeholders will also make use of the interview as opportunity to gather information about the market, especially if the candidates are from competitor companies.

5. **Compliance**- Yes, the candidate is frequently accessed for compliance. This also ties in with point 2, which is about not bringing potential problem to the Stakeholders. It is not just about the potential to outshine the boss one day, it is also about whether the person can respect the authority of the supervisor and the other seniors, and whether the person will abide to the code of conduct, ethics, policies, rules (written and hidden), security, legalities, and any business-related/trade compliance.

6. **Credentials**- This really depends on the nature of the job position, as well as the industry. More often than not, most hirers tend to skip the education and awards

part of the resume and not bother with them as long as they meet minimal requirement (in which case the HR should have already vetted them), but sometimes it may not be the case. For senior roles within the technical sector, a PhD is stringently examined for its credibility, and they sometimes count the impact factor of published journals. For most of academia and government sectors, they will bother about which schools the candidates came from.

With the above to ponder about, the resourceful candidate should be able to come up with a game plan that will precisely target these (psychological) factors to turn the interview in favor towards increased successes. The game plan however will not work, if the candidates cannot even get the message across. Remember, as I mentioned a while ago, the whole point of the interview is to clear doubt, and how the adoption of the right persona will therefore steer the candidate in the right direction, which is what I'll be talking about next.

Creating an Interview Persona

While the psychology of the interviewers largely remains the same, the ways to approach the different types of interviewers will still greatly differ. I have stressed before that adaptability is the key to success in the interview process, and the Darwinian quote best sums up the essence of this message, "It is not the most intellectual or the strongest of species that survives; but the species that survives is the one that is able to adapt to and adjust best to the changing environment in which it finds itself." The best qualification and the best (most impressive) interview may not guarantee you the job. It tends to go to one who is the most adaptable in creating an effective interview persona to clear doubts and offer value proposition.

Some readers may find this approach troubling, because you would prefer to stay true to yourself or remain honest, and do not want to put up a fake persona, especially if it will get exposed after you get the job. But you must understand one thing- the working world does not appreciate your true self. It is a world that is primarily veiled by forms, and the substances are secondary. Every successful professional has a work persona, and that itself is respected, because a sensible person will keep public/work life and personal life separate. And also, the whole point of using the interview persona is to get you through the interviews, and even if you'll revert back to more natural state later, there's not much anyone can do about it because you already got the job. Remember, in order to get the job, you have to get through the interview first. The winner is counted as someone with the job, and not who is a "genuine" person.

The interview persona is something which requires a good amount of **research**. There are four steps in the research.

1. **Understanding the Industry**- You have to identify the nature of your industry, which will tell much about how your work environment will be like. For example, are you planning to move into a banking sector? What will the people from the banking sector be like? Meticulous, posh and insincere, with high turnover? Take note of all these points.

2. **Researching the Company**- Now, start deep diving into the company you're applying to. The simplest way is to look at the employee's reviews on Glassdoor, and read all the good and bad ones to form a certain idea about its culture. Do you think it will be a cultural fit for your personality? And if you really want the job, do you think you are capable of adapting an interview, and subsequently a professional persona to take up the challenges? Are you able to speak their lingos or at least copy them? When you're at it, do research and try to figure out the current pain-points of the company if they are any. Try to find out some **likely solutions** for the **pain-points**, make a mental note of them, and use them appropriately throughout the interview process.

3. **Researching on the Job**- Take the job descriptor and try to understand the nature of your role. Is it an operational, commercial or technical role? Is this a replacement position or a newly created one? Will you be interacting with other departments? Are you a solo contributor or have reporting lines? And who are you going to be reporting to in your job- who is your boss?

4. **Checking the Profiles**- And very importantly, do snoop on the profiles of the interviewers; the bosses/decision makers, or other people who might be involved (like the HR, other employees). The best way to do so is via LinkedIn, and when possible, on other social media platform. See their faces and get a gut feel. Take a look at their professional life, and also their social life when possible, and try to figure what kind of person they are.

After you go through the four steps, you can apply the second part, which is to form the **expectations** from your research findings. As a general rule, if your interviewers are from the academia, they tend to like candidates who serve as echo chambers; meaning to say, in agreement with their work. If the interviewers are from a more commercial outfit, they like to see highly positive, energetic candidates. If the interviewers work in more operational and regulatory settings, they like candidates who appear more complicit, stable (thus boring) and meticulous. And when the interviewers are from technical outfit, they prefer candidates who are factual, logical and precise.

After knowing what the expectations are going to be like, the next part is to identify potential **trigger** points. Triggers are things which can bring displeasure to the interviewers, and therefore you'll consciously not want to step on those potential landmines. Here are some general triggers: for the interviewers from academia, they tend not to like candidates who have antithetical opinions about their work. They are hiring candidates to enable their work to become more successful and gain higher credentials. For interviewers from commercial outfit, they tend not to like candidates who do not seem to have the 'drive', yet they will dislike more the candidates who are too over eager to shine, or even possibly outshine them, if they are too competent. People from the commercial outfit usually tend to be the most political, and because of that they frequently work their way up to senior management. For interviewers from operational/regulatory settings, they are highly cautious of candidates who seem to display tendencies to be divergent, or negligent, for fear of disruption/hijack in their work function. And lastly, interviewers from technical outfit do not like histrionics typical of people from the commercial setting, lack or inadequacy of technical knowledge, and displays of logical inconsistencies.

To sum up all of the above, there are essentially three parts to the creation of an interview persona. The first part is research of the interviewers, the second part is expectation of the interviewers, and finally, the third part is identifying trigger points to avoid. Do consciously tailor your interview persona accordingly and you should be able to then have a more effective interview with increased chances towards success.

Three-Pronged Selling

I have discussed about the psychology of hiring, and also touched on the creation of interview persona. Now, let's lay down a plan which will summarily incorporate the above. I call this the "Three-Pronged Selling" approach. Yes, some readers may not have sales experience, or feel uncomfortable with the idea of selling, yet this is so very vital in the interview process, because the whole idea is to sell yourself during the interview. And in order for the hirers to buy into you, you must create compelling reasons on why you are the best for the job- better than all the rest of the other candidates. This sales process is actually not difficult; you just have to study ways to carry out the three prongs simultaneously during the interviews, namely: **Fitting In**, **Clearing of Doubts**, and **Value Proposition**.

1. **Fitting In**, as the name suggests, is to put you on a comfortable level with the interviewers. The very first thing that anybody need to do is to **be friendly, behave courteous and act appropriately**, which is something most normal adults are capable of. This will clear the first hurdle, regarding **the general sense of the attitude**. This is further aided by employing the **Interview Persona**.

   Let's reiterate, there are three parts of the Interview Persona, namely, **research**, **expectations**, **triggers**.

Within research, the four steps to do so is: to **understand the industry**, **research the company**, **research on the job**, and **studying the profiles of the interviewers**. From within research, you'll have also unraveled the **pain-points** as well as the **likely solutions** which will be useful later, and keep a mental note on that. The research finding will flow into laying down the expectations of your conversation with the interviewers, and also help you to identify trigger points which you will consciously avoid in order not to screw up the conversation.

The whole point of all these steps is to clear at least three barriers of disapproval, which are **prejudice and bias**, **culture fit**, and **threats**. It also addresses the thoughts in the hirers' mind, which are **ability to solve problems and not cause problems**, as well as **compliance** (this is in term of agreeability).

2. **Clearing of Doubts** is a major work in the whole interview processes. The whole point of the interview is to clear away doubts surrounding the candidate's experiences and capability, if not the resumes will simply suffice and then there's no need to do so. The use of the Interview Persona will certainly improve the situation when the candidate can enable a comfortable level of discussion with the interviewers. But there are the five Cs to work on here.

a) **Competency**- The person needs to show the very basis of the hire, the possession of the right competency (skillsets) for the job. The competency that is reflected on the resume needs to be verified through probes and questions like knowledge about certain skillsets and/or industries. This is made to address several points: **veracity of the information**, **ability to solve problems and not cause problems**, and **value and affordability**.

b) **Claims**- Are you able to back up any of your claims? Basically any evidence or proof of claims (certifications, transcripts, recommendations from employers) which ties in to additional points to address like **credentials** and **compliance** (this is in term of professional certs for compliance related roles) on top of the points already mentioned in competency. Such evidences may also help address the question on **potential problems with hire**.

c) **Clarity**- Be clear and concise about what you want to share. When your messages become unintelligible, it is difficult for the hirers to do **summary building and notes taking** and/or **opportunity to gather info**. By being clear and concise, you make the hirers life easier, and they'll surely appreciate you for that. When a person is not clear or concise, it sometimes becomes an indicator about the candidate's (lack of) intelligence or communication skills, which will raise questions in **ability to solve problems and not create**

problems, as well as **potential problems with hire**. If you're not particularly good in talking or framing a thought, then try to slow down and speak in point forms, so long as your points are effectively conveyed.

d) **Consistency**- You'd jolly well make sure that you do not deviate from what is on the resume and what you're going to say in the interview. Make sure that the accounts are consistent. Likewise, this also applies the same during interviews; make sure what you now remain consistent with what had been said ten minutes ago. Transgression of this rule will raise every red flag conceivable especially on **veracity of the information**, because they will think that the candidates are lying and/or couldn't remember their lies.

e) **Conscientiousness**- It's not just about appearing friendly, courteous and acting appropriately, it is also about the notion that the candidate will be able to do one's work responsibly and dutifully, which addresses the points in **ability to solve problems and not create problems, general sense of the attitude**, and even about **value and affordability**. The candidate can do so by hinting at commitments and work appreciation in previous roles and the ex-bosses' approvals.

3. **Value Proposition**- The last prong should be carefully thought through and carried out. To propose the appropriate value, the candidate should first be reminded about the **pain-points** as well as **likely solutions** that were gathered from the research work during the building of the interview persona. By consciously dropping hints of the likely solutions during the interview (at appropriate opportunities), it will certainly add to the value you can put forth.

There are also other things which you can carefully use to augment your pre-existing qualities, and add to the expectations of the job role. These are known as **additional value-adds**. They should not be boastful, unrealistic, and they should also be non-threatening to the interviewers. The value-adds should be something which makes the interviewer feel like they're getting some advantage and benefit out of hiring you, rather than to feel shortchanged, or threatened. It can also be something which can imply that your addition will make their jobs easier or career more successful. The best type of value which you should put forth is a skill or knowledge which is not existing in the current department/organization, but also not of sufficient power to displace the authority. For example, a candidate for a sales role can value add by claiming knowledge about the competitors of the hiring company. Or a candidate for a digital marketing role can add value by claiming skillsets with SEO optimization.

By proposing value proposition to the hirers, you'll likely address the questions on **value and affordability**, **budget**, and even fulfil the hirers' **hope to get the right one**. These value propositions should set yourself apart from other candidates and give the interviewers compelling reasons to hire you.

During the interview processes, the three-pronged selling of yourself should be applied constantly, and also appropriately. Do time yourself, especially when it comes to value proposition, so as not to appear too overly eager or desperate. It certainly helps if the candidate has some ideas about the general flow and scheme of a normal interview, so you'll be able anticipate the opportune timepoints in advance.

The Flow of a Typical Interview

The reason why I can lay down the flow of a typical interview is because most interviewers follow an almost textbook-like methodology in questions and answers. There are essentially three parts of a typical interview, namely **laying down of expectations**, **gathering of information**, and **interrogation**. I also mark * for key section where the candidate can inject value proposition to stir the interests of the interviewer.

1. The typical interview begins with formalities like greetings, and maybe short small talks before it proceeds to the serious part.

2. After the formalities, the interviewer will usually mention about what the company stands for, job descriptors, as well as responsibilities (laying down of expectations), before asking if there are any questions for him or her. It may get a little tough when they ask a question like, "what do you think of our company?" (interrogation). The interviewer may also begin instead with asking the candidate to give an introduction about himself/herself, as well as a summary of past work experiences (gathering of information). Do note that you should not get too carried away with talking about yourself and past work experiences, because most interviewers would prefer to get to the main points for

them to take note than to hear the candidates continually ramble on. *

3. The kind of questions the interviewer tends to ask in the beginning are about why the candidate left the last job, or choose to join this company (interrogation).

4. If there are any need for further clarifications on skillsets or past experiences, the interviewer will certainly press on (interrogation). But most interviewers will probably move on to ask the candidates to highlight specific achievements that were most notable in the past experiences (gathering of information). The interviewer may also ask about what are the ways the candidates employ to get those achievements (interrogation). *

5. Most interviewers at this point will go deeper into the job responsibilities (laying down of expectations), and also test the responses of the candidates by asking questions pertaining to such job responsibilities (interrogation).*

6. At this point (usually from pass the midpoint of the interview), do anticipate difficult questions which tend to stump many interviewees, like "what's your five-year plans?", "can you tell me your greatest weaknesses?" (interrogation).

7. When most of the questionings by the interviewers are done, the interviewer will then ask if the candidates

have any questions to ask in turn. This is usually not innocuous as it sounds, because it is yet another test on the candidates (interrogation).

8. Nearer to the end of the interview, the interviewer will give the standard SOP statement about the HR process on follow-up and notification should the candidate get chosen for the next round (laying down of expectations). The conversation may gradually steer into small talks before ending, but may also end abruptly at this point.

Sometimes the interviews may not follow through similar sequences, but the idea is basically there. There will always be the three parts prevalent at any point in the discussion. As the readers probably sense so, the most challenging parts lie in interrogation. In order to do well, the second prong in the three-pronged selling strategy, which is the Clearing of Doubts, is crucial in mitigating the interrogation, because this is where most of the doubts and "entrapments" are laid down in the interview process.

It is also a process which is determinative for surviving the interview round. On the other hand, in sections that are marked *, the candidate may use the third prong in the three-pronged selling strategy, which is the Value Proposition to engineer interests at the hirers side, towards more favorable outcome.

Be Careful of One-Way Interview

With the advent of technology, as well as the growing need to bring time/cost savings and increase efficiencies, many interviews these days are carried out online by virtual interview. Most of these interviews facilitate meeting of hiring manager and candidates through video software and platform, rather than the traditional face-to-face meeting, which have become the standard for most job hiring processes, especially in times of social distancing like the recent pandemic for instance.

But there are also many interviews that are conducted by pre-recorded questions without the physical participation of the interviewers. This type of virtual interview is termed one-way interview, and as the name implies, is a one-way street for the candidates, whereby the candidates will not be actually participating in conversation with the interviewers, but pre-recorded videos.

Such interviews are deemed useful for the companies, who will probably benefit from the structured process, and the filtering algorithms that come bundled with the software. These interviews can also be sent to multiple candidates without compromising the available time of the interviewers. Unfortunately, these methods have brought about additional challenges to the average candidates.

In preparation for such one-way interviews, the interviewers will pre-record a series of questions in the video, and have them put into different intervals within the interviews. A selected candidate will usually be notified of such an arrangement via an email, with a link for the candidate to download the software and install on their computers, a link that bring to a page explaining the processes, as well as practice rounds for them to get prepared, as well as a link for the actual interview at a specific date and time.

When the interview process begins, the pre-recorded questions will be played out, and the candidates will be given specific time to answer through video recording, with no chance to pause or rewind/re-record, but is allowed to skip the questions (and there's no returning to skipped questions though).

Since the candidates are constrained into a tight schedule, with no way to undo and redo the interviews, they are really put into a tight spot. Despite ample preparations, the candidates may still find it hard to properly express themselves and cover the key points, because most people are used to human conversations than with a virtual machine. For that reason, the one-way interviews have to be handled extremely carefully, as it may severely jeopardize qualified and competent candidates who performed badly during such interviews.

One of the best ways to handle such a daunting task is to actually prepare a list of potential questions and answers, and keep practicing via the computer (the best way is to turn the camera on and speak to it while visualizing how you look and behave). The most usual questions are, "what do you understand about our company?", "introduce yourself and list your past experiences", "highlight your achievements in your career", "how would you react if you face a certain problem at your job?" and "how will you contribute in this role you are applying to?" When you are preparing your answers to some of these questions, highlight key points, which may be the key factors matching the job requirement, as well as your perceived value propositions to the company.

Do write all of them down on a sheet of paper, with those key points highlighted in a bright, distinctive color. Then do practice run and time yourself (each answer interval will probably last between 1 to 5 minutes). When you begin the session, have the sheet of paper for ready reference.

Knowing that there are filtering algorithms which will process the recorded sessions, it is important to be very clear and concise when bringing up the key points during the interview. The software will pick up specific keywords and undergo a matching process to calculate the eligibility of the candidate. Afterwards, it will generate a report to the interviewers for their considerations of the different profiles that had undergone these interviews.

To summarize the ways to succeed in these one-way interviews, always remember to have ample practices, to have key points readily available for easy reference, to speak clearly and intelligibly, and very importantly, try not to be anxious and fumble through the recordings.

Rules of Engagement

I've said enough about things that the candidates ought to do and say to increase their chances during the interviews. Now I'll talk about things that should not be said or should never be attempted. I have included here a list of topics that are off limit in the discussion during interviews, and while they are common-sensical, sometimes they are not when candidates get overly excited and blurted them out.

1. **Do not ask salary at the outset**- You simply don't talk about the salary that early in the conversation, unless the interviewers initiate it. Usually there should be a salary already indicated in the job descriptors, but if there are none, you should try to get a sense of the market rate before even proceeding to apply. Once you are in the interview, do not enquire about the salary for a number of reasons- you're not even hired yet, so you have no right to begin the negotiation process, and you'll also be seen as someone who is only in it for the money (yes, isn't that what job is all about, to get money?), because the objective of the companies is to get someone to help them to make money, and not the other way round.

2. **Do not say bad things about previous employers**- The last employers could have been mean to you, or you think that they suck, but still, you should never criticize your former employers- company, department,

the boss, the people and the work. This is one thing that will almost get the interviewer to immediately dislike you, because if you can do that to the last organization, you can also potentially do the same to this one. Do not share your grievances even if you've suffered injustice, but stay objective and professional.

3. **Do not give real reasons for bad departure**- Maybe you were terminated from the last job. But to bring up this will certainly cast a negative light on you. Resignations and even retrenchments (getting laid off due to company restructuring) are actually not so bad and understandable; you can creatively use them as reasons for your departure. But termination has negative connotations associated with incompetency, and personal flaws (disagreeability, inability to work as a team, bad attitude).

4. **Do not downplay the importance of anyone, including yourself**- Maybe you're asked for your opinions regarding the industry, companies, people, practices and type of work, and you may be very opinionated about them, but do not downplay their importance, or criticize them, because you'll be seen as somewhat conceited. And likewise, do not downplay your own achievements, because self-deprecation is a kind of false modesty that will not bring you respect. While you're conscious of not trying to impress too much during the interview, you should also be mindful of not putting yourself down.

5. **Do not reveal company information**- You are not obliged to share too much about your previous or current company to a new company especially when you are not even hired yet. Sometimes the candidates thought that this is a positive gesture to the potential hirer, to give them valuable information or to appear transparent, but this is actually a very dangerous move, which can even potentially lead to lawsuits if you're not careful. And also, the interviewers may find such candidates a bit of a snitch and turncoat. Yet, they throw these questions all the time because they do certainly get benefits from such information. One of the most common tricks used by the interviewers is to ask a salesperson about how much he or she have achieved in the portfolio in the last or current job, in terms of revenue. If you're ever asked such a question, be careful not to give any quantifiable amount, and instead be professional and either quote a rough estimate of the percentage in the addressable market, or tell them that it is not right for you to do so that early in the interview, and that you will gladly share them once you are officially in the role.

6. **Do not make unrealistic claims**- While you'd certainly like to play up your value, you should be careful not to make unrealistic claims, especially for public projects that you are not credited for. As industry insiders, some of the interviewers may know a thing or two about the projects that your last company undertake. If you really have a part to play in a certain project, albeit a small contribution, you'd have to carefully craft your claim to

make it look like you're an important player, while at the same time, buffering the impact by saying things that might even score you brownie points, something like, "I've made significant contribution in this project that are appreciated by my team mates, but at the end of the day, I am privileged to be in a very excellent team."

7. **Do not appear overconfident**- Most interviewers do not like braggarts, especially when they appear insubstantial. Candidates who sought advices from other career consultants may overcompensate on impressing the interviewers by putting up ridiculous amount of confidence, both in the way they carry themselves, as well as the things they say. Sometimes the candidates even thought that outwitting the interviewer or playing the wise guy is a clever thing, whereby instead it's a most stupid thing to do. While braggarts are just harmless clowns, on the other hand, the candidates who appear too impressive in their credentials may also become a threat to the interviewers, due to the perceived ability to do work better than the latter (thus becoming a potential threat for the person's job). The best approach for the candidate to take, is to present themselves with a certain amount of modesty, which is not about assuming a weak position, but behaving in a measured manner that exude quiet confidence and agreeability.

8. **Do not veer into controversies**- Sometimes the interview may diverge into more personal discussions. At this point, do not relax your guard and turn into a loose cannon. You may have interesting opinions

about certain topics concerning politics, race, religion, gender, but these things should be strictly kept off limit in all interviews, because they can cause lasting damages to your reputation if the other camp is in disagreement. It is not professional to share such controversial opinions, since the job market largely remains politically correct.

9. **Do not overstep boundaries**- Sure, you had a great time with the interviewer. But you wouldn't want to overstep boundary and try to go buddy-buddy with the interviewer, because the professional relationship, as well as the authority still remains, especially when the interviewer is going to be your potential boss in the future. Do not think that by being over-friendly is going to win the interviewer to your side as a friend and help you to get express pass towards securing the job, because it most likely will not work. Do not think that flattery and brown-nosing will also get you anywhere, because most interviewers are conscious about such antics, and will probably see you in a bad light, especially if you over-do them.

10. **Do not dominate conversation**- During the interview, do not talk more than necessary, and always listen more than you speak, to allow the interviewers ample time to finish their sentences and ask questions. Do not try to dominate the conversation, and worse, interrupt the interviewers. When you transgress on this rule, the interviewers will consciously or subconsciously dislike you even though they may not say it.

Take Note of Subtle Cues

Candidates will often try to judge the outcome of the interview by getting a sense of the different cues dropped by the interviewers along the way. While greater positive cues certainly count towards increasing the successes of the interview, it may still not eventually guarantee a job.

When taking note of subtle cues, the candidates should dispel the notion that this therefore counts towards any guarantee, but rather consider them as indicators to gauge and steer the course of the conversation accordingly. Positive cues are encouraging for candidates to pursue the conversation down that similar direction, while negative cues should serve as reminder for the candidates to not continue to pursue down that path, and to carefully steer the conversation back into its original course.

Below are several subtle cues that the candidates will encounter in interviews from time to time. These cues are divided between positive, negative and neutral cues.

1. **Disapproval** (Negative)- When the interviewer shows certain signs of disapproval, like raised eyebrow (doubt), frown (dissatisfaction), shaking of head (disbelief) and even going on the offensive (displeasure), the candidate should take heed and either stop going down that course, or try to mitigate

this disapproval by remediation through positive justification (to give valid reasons for the statement than to make it sound like excuses), or through diversion (to steer the unpleasant part into more comfortable territory). Sometimes the best diversion is to suddenly break the disapproval by injecting a strong positive and appealing statement for redemption.

2. **Impatience** (Negative)- Signs of impatience- yawning, fidgeting or impatient tone, often have little to do with time constraints and urgency, but rather time wasted in the interviewer's opinion. When the interviewer displays impatience, it signals to the candidates one of several things: either what was said is not clear or concise, or the conversation is too slow, uninteresting, long-winded, or largely dominated by the candidate for too long. After receiving such signals, the first thing the candidate should do is to pause the conversation, then courteously ask the interviewer if there are questions about what had been said, and express the willingness to ratify them when necessary.

3. **Abrupt End** (Negative)- When there's supposed to be a good amount of time left in the interview, and yet the interviewers decide to end the interview quickly and abruptly, chances are they might have already lost interest with the candidates. At this juncture, the candidate should attempt at least to try once to see if this interest can be renewed by injecting a very strong and interesting point into the conversation, but if that still doesn't work out, then it's time to just follow along and end the conversation.

4. **Lack of Note Taking** (Negative)- When you find interviewers not taking any notes about what the candidates say, it's usually a clear sign of lack of interest, and they will simply just go through the motion until the interview finishes (they will usually try to cut short the meeting).

5. **Urgency** (Neutral)- When the interviewers seem to rush through time, or keep staring at the watch/clock while talking, chances are they are in a bit of rush, to get this interview quickly finished with all points covered (different from ending abruptly), because they could have busy work ahead. This is a neutral cue, as it has nothing to do with the candidates.

6. **Expressing Interest** (Neutral)- Most of the western world is polite and diplomatic, so the interviewers may try to get the candidates comfortable and assured by saying positive, encouraging things and implying interests. However, one should only take this at face value, because it's not a gesture that will definitely lead one to get a job; it's just a friendly (and insincere) expression, unless the interviewers explicitly tell the candidates that they want to hire them.

7. **Taking Down of Notes** (Neutral)- While not taking notes is a negative cue, note taking is not exactly a positive cue, but still a more neutral cue, because any conscientious interviewers would need to do so, so they can build up a report for their superiors, or use them for their own references.

8. **Talkative Interviewers** (Neutral/Positive)- An interviewer who yaks non-stop and appears high energy may not necessarily be indicative of a positive cue. This interviewer may simply be a person who just happen to enjoy talking. But rest assure that in most cases, if the interviewer displays this level of enthusiasm, it's still rather encouraging for the candidates, which makes then interviews tilt slightly towards the positive side.

9. **Showing Interest in Personal Aspects** (Positive)- When the interviewer displays an interest in the more personal aspects of the candidates, from asking about social life, family, to hobbies, this is usually a rather positive cue because this means that the interviewer is showing interest in the candidate and would like to know more about the person. By all mean, the candidate should take advantage of this welcoming gesture from the interviewer and encourage them to go ahead.

10. **Willingness to Establish Further Contacts** (Positive)- One of the very positive cue the candidate can pick up from the interviewer is when the latter initiate to establish further contacts, either through sharing personal numbers to the candidate, or make suggestions for catchups (of non-interview nature) over coffee. This is usually indicative of comfort and approval with the candidate, and when there are such opportunities, the candidate should gladly oblige.

Questions and Answers

The main reason why most people are afraid of interviews lies in the difficult questions that are frequently asked. Some of the questions may even seem to be purposely designed for the sake of putting the candidates in a tough spot, where any sort of reply will not put them in any better light. But that is precisely why this sort of questions are asked; to reveal any inconsistencies, red flags and resourcefulness per the interviewee. Below is a list of frequently encountered questions, with their main objectives and purposes revealed, and also with the most appropriate ways they can be answered.

1. **Tell me about yourself?** – The interviewer should already have some idea about the candidate through the resume; this question serves to find any inconsistencies between what's been said and written, and also to test out the confidence, articulation and how the candidate's mind works- if he or she can organize and summarize the experiences, and verbalize it in a structured manner.

   Answer: Always make sure that your verbal account matches the ones in your resume. Do not be too long-winded, but do make sure that you are able to cover the main points in a structured, concise and summarized manner. A good flow should start with you talking about where you are currently right now (if not, about the last job), how your career is a culmination of certain type of experience needed by the company while looking retrospectively at what had been done, and then filling in the experiences from the previous companies in snapshot with highlights in those places. Do pause when you've rambled a bit and prompt the interviewer for any questions before you continue.

2. **How would you describe yourself in one word? –** The question is asked to elicit certain information pertaining to your personality, how confident you are in self-perception, and how this adjective can contribute to the given role.

   Answer: Do be wary of the fact that not all positive adjectives work well with the interviewers. You should already have a good idea about the culture and the type of person you are dealing with when you are building an interview persona for this job. Customize your adjective and apply it accordingly. For example, you wouldn't want to use the word "creative" for an accounting job.

3. **Why do you want to join this company? –** This question is intended to find out about what drives you most, how well you've researched the company, and how much you want this job. Clearly you apply to this role because you want the job, but how you prioritize them reveals what is most important to you.

Answer: The key to succeeding in this answer lies in the extent you've researched the company and the job, and the identification of its positive traits which motivate you enough to really want this job. Be careful of sounding desperate, insufficient knowledge about the company or role and having wrong or undesirable priorities (looking for higher pay, wanting to leave bad boss, getting express career progression).

4. **Why do you want to leave your current/last job?** – The interviewers may want to identify any potential red flags and issues the candidate can potentially bring to the table. They may try to determine whether you've had difficulty working with people or your current/previous jobs, and whether you're someone who is easily bored/irresponsible and/or a frequent job hopper.

   Answer: Do not say anything negative about anybody, even if it may really be the case. Anything negative said would almost certainly backfire and sink your chances of securing the job. Rather, try to put forth reasons that actually sound positive, and would even be of benefit to the organization, like, about you wanting to seek more challenging positions.

5. **Tell me something good/bad about your current/last roles?** – This question is some kind of entrapment on the candidate, because the interviewer is out to test the propensity for disloyalty and indiscretion in the candidate. Anyone who is capable of talking bad about other employers, regardless of

whether the bad parts are factual or not, is likely to repeat and do the same to this employer.

Answer: Faced with a question like that, the candidate should only consciously focus on the good things in the current/last role. If the candidate is egged on by the interviewer to say something bad, the candidate should either try to turn the negative part into something like different job expectations/job fits with the employer, or stand his/her ground and say something like, "Sorry, but I am afraid I can't do this, as it will be unprofessional of me to do so."

6. **What are your strengths/weaknesses?** – The question is designed to enable the interviewer to gather red flags, deal breakers and find out if there's inability of the candidate to work well with other people. Either way, both answers may serve to sabotage you if not carefully answered. By talking about your strengths, they can be seen as potential threat by insecure hirers, especially if they have lack of them. By talking about weaknesses, you are exposing your negative traits, which may jeopardize the prospect of the career.

Answer: You should try to tread carefully both strengths and weaknesses and turn them into assets for the company. The strength should be complementary and applicable to the new role, and non-threatening to the potential bosses. Whereas, the weaknesses should have a silver lining, the minor types which are common in most people, and which may even serve the hirer. Some examples of weaknesses which may become assets to the employers: obsessive compulsive attitude towards details to make sure work is properly done with no allowance for errors, and incessantly taking care of feelings of other colleagues because you value harmony in the work environment.

7. **How do you see yourself in 5 years time?** – This is a classic trick question which is served to check on the ambition of the candidate. If this question is asked in the context of joining this company, then it definitely will be indicative of how far the candidate would like to climb the career ladder within this organization, and whether this candidate has the audacity to want to go too far ahead (thus threatening the boss) and even turn disloyal (though this is not an indicator of disloyalty; there will be other tests to do so).

Answer: Faced with a question like this, the candidate may face a dilemma and a potential catch-22- by stating great ambition, like becoming the manager, the candidate may raise potential red flag, and by downplaying the next 5 years with modesty, it may become self-deprecating and lacking in confidence. The best answer to handle this question is to say something along the line of, "I hope to get this job, and keep improving at this job, to become a better worker of this job over the next 5 years."

8. **Have you ever wanted to become an entrepreneur?**
   – Another trick question, this one may indicate whether the candidate can be a potential flight risk, or even a competitor-in-the-making in the future.

   Answer: If you had already experience in entrepreneurship, you can simply state that it's all been done, and you realize that it's not for you. If you do not have prior experiences, simply say no, you're not interested, as you'll prefer to be gainfully employed in this company of your choosing.

9. **Out of all the candidates, why should we hire you?**
   – You see, the irony of this question is that you don't know who are the other candidates. But when this question is asked, it is really meant to give you the opportunity to put forth your value proposition, to say a bunch of things for you to sell yourself. On the other hand, it could also be a sign that you're not performing up to expectation, and you need to catch up.

   Answer: Consider that the comparison is for something which is beyond what the job descriptor and expectations entail, because most candidates should more or less meet those requirements. The extra thing you input should pertain to additional skillsets, exceptional work ethics, and other qualities. If it the question is directed at you in a more negative manner, you'd need to step up and put forth more qualities about yourself to the interviewer.

10. **How did you make time for this interview?** – Most job interviews take place during office hours on weekdays, and the interviewers know that, but sometimes they would like to see how working employees are able to take time off to attend the interview. This can more or less tell them about the candidate's integrity as an employee.

Answer: You'd almost certainly want the interviewers to know that the interview takes place during your breaks, or on your leave days (though not sick leave as you're not supposed to malinger). Try to convince the interviewers that you've made sufficient preparation to treat your current job as first priority, followed by the interview.

11. **How do you handle difficult colleague or boss in your current/last role?** – Notice the subliminal tone within this question, it is meant to imply that you have difficult colleagues or bosses to begin with. The interviewer may want you to blurt out something negative regarding your relationship with these colleagues, so as to ascertain your inability to get well with the rest in the new organization you're applying to.

Answer: Firstly, you should lay down a disclaimer that while there are certainly disagreements anyway (it's a part and parcel of the working world), so far you think that your boss and colleagues are not that difficult to work with. Secondly, you should try to illustrate some scenarios about how you properly handle certain disagreements, reaching out for conciliatory win-win moves kept in the utmost professionalism while doing so.

12. **What are you most proud of in your current/last role?** - This question is a test of passion, conviction, articulation, and competency. It is assumed that if you can speak with such enthusiasm, passion and eloquence about your past project, you'd probably be able to do the same when you do it on behalf of this company.

Answer: Do articulate well, and foster positive energy when you share one of the most important highlights of your career. Consciously take note that this is a chance to shine, to showcase your value proposition towards the interviewer. Do practice on specific keywords and terms that will be well received by the other side.

13. **Can you tell me the (sensitive info) about your current/last company?** - This question serves two purpose: one is to learn more about your current/last company as part of market intelligence gathering, the other is to test the propensity of you selling out a company, and worst still, breaching confidentiality and intellectual property.

Answer: The straight answer is no, but to be said in a courteous manner like, "I am really sorry, but I cannot agree to your request, as I am bound by non-disclosure of such information by my company, which I have to respect and abide with."

14. **Tell me about a time you made a mistake?** – While everyone makes mistakes, the interviewer would like to find out if there's any mistake that you made in the past that would become too costly for this organization to bear. The interviewer can also learn how you apply your resourcefulness when trying to solve problems.

    Answer: Make sure that you are quoting a mistake that is not costly or serious, and which will actually hint at your positive work ethics. And also ensure that you are coupling the mistake with a remedy that should go to your credit. For example, you could quote an example on some mistakes you made in the email when you were working overtime (hence tired), late into the night while rushing through a project, but was promptly notified the next day because you tend to save your emails to review with your colleagues to ensure consensus before sending, so you could ratify them before they got out.

15. **Are you also looking at other opportunities?** - There's nothing wrong with looking at other opportunities, and if the candidate says otherwise, there's a good chance that he or she is lying. Therefore, the interviewer will sometimes throw this question at the candidate to assess the trustworthiness.

    Answer: When asked about it, simply say yes you are. If you've been jobless for a while, and you still yes to this, it might create an impression that you've been looking at opportunities for a long time, but that's what it really is. You can simply try to cover track by explaining away that your job search began only quite recently, and gives justification on why it took such a long time for you to begin the search, which will be addressed in the next question/answer.

16. **Why was there a gap?** – It can be quite disconcerting to be asked such a question. Those periods of unemployment may happen due to a variety of reasons, but the interviewers would surely want to know, because they tend to become skeptical with candidates who had been out of the job market for too long, or had huge gaps between jobs in the resumes. They are usually concerned that there might be some undesirable elements involved with the candidates that result in this lack of success in securing jobs.

    Answer: Well, I've previously discussed that it is possible to fill the gap and cover the tracks, by coming up with a 'valid excuse', like having a registered entity to claim that you've been involved in entrepreneurship for a while. Otherwise, an education is also a good way to justify those gaps. If you've none of them, the best answer to give is to simply tell the interviewer that you've private family matters to attend to during that period, and chances are they will not probe further and/or even feel some sympathy and respect for you.

17. **Why did you stay for such a short time at that job/several jobs?** – This is a tricky question for those who had short stints in some organizations. It may be indicative of bad performance and wrong job fit. The

interviewers would be especially concerned if most of the past experiences are like that, because that's usually a sign of a job-hopper, and they surely wouldn't like such flighty addition to their headcounts.

Answer: Be prepared to come up with a good excuse for that. If it happens early in the career, you can try to say that you were still trying to find yourself back then, and you've came a long way since. If it happens very often, you can try to explain that you were in a particularly bad period of your life and was trying to handle difficult personal matters, but now all is resolved, and you're willing to be committed in this new role. If it happens in one particular company, just explain away that there's a genuine job mismatch, and that did not happen again.

18. **Assuming you get employed, what can we expect from you in the first three months?** – When the employers ask such a question, they probably want to get a sense of how much the candidates understand about this role, and how they can proactively plan and structure their work.

Answers: Through the research you gathered when building up the interview persona, you should have a good idea about what the job entails. Make use of this information, divide up the 3 months and imagine how you can apply your skillsets to cumulatively grow from month to month. Try not to make huge leaps when you describe the stages, but plan it in a reasonable way which is realistic yet challenging enough. Do not worry about setting expectations on whatever you say here, because the interviewers will likely not remember them later.

19. **What do you like to do outside of work?** - While this question may sound more casual and personable (which is indeed a positive cue), do not relax your guard at all, because the interviewer is trying to get to know more about you as a person and would try to get a sense of your personality through your social life to apply it into the working life, as well as the amount of family commitment you undertake, so they can get an idea on how well you can balance with work commitment.

    Answer: Try not to sound extravagant or crazy about your life outside work, especially in a conservative organization. You can talk about normal hobbies and routine, but what the interviewers are probably more interested to know about are any unusual aspects about you, and how you handle family commitment and time spent.

20. **What questions do you have for me?** – At this point, the interviewer offers up a chance for the candidate to ask questions (and also to take a break from asking questions), but it may also turn out to be a way for them to assess the interest level as well as the attentiveness of the candidate.

    Answer: When given the chance to ask questions, the candidate should try to ask the right questions, that are appropriate, sensible and professional. Take note of the rules of engagement to avoid transgressing on off limit questions and comments. Some of the better questions to ask (if they are not already stated) are: what is the timeline of hire, which departments will we constantly interact with, are there any new developments in the company.

While not the most exhaustive list on every question asked, most questions you'd expect to find in interviews tend to revolve around the above formats. The candidates should take heed to handle them appropriately, and try their best to give the best answer possible. However, be mindful that while the questions can be skillfully answered, they may not necessarily increase the chances of success of the candidates. Candidates who did not answer the questions well enough may still get the job at the end. And likewise, candidates who seem to answer everything perfectly may still not get the job.

Remember, the whole point of this interview is to clear doubts (therefore be careful when your answers sound inconsistent or increase doubt), and not a contest for the most talented communicator (unless it's for a job that requires that). Sometimes, the candidates who appear too clever in answering all questions perfectly may seem seasoned or practiced, and interviewers who are on lookout for the perfect slave may not like that. Still, it pretty much depends on the kind of company, person and setting that are in the interview, which should be pretty telling when you've done enough research when you're building up the interview persona.

Following Up After Interview

So, you've nailed that interview. But that's not the end. There are several things you'll need to follow up on, and whatever you do here may still count towards improving your chances at securing the job.

The interviewers will usually set certain expectations for the candidates before ending the interviews. Most of the time they will state a timeline to review the other candidates and for consideration/selection, before they could definitely update you on their decisions, either on the hiring or future rounds of interviews. They may not always stick to their proposed schedule when the process is delayed or when the candidates are no longer held in consideration though.

At that point, it is important to get them to suggest a date that you can take note of and check back with them for updates. If they cannot give an actual date, then do ask for estimated timeline in weeks. When you have gotten the date or timeline available, take note of it to use it for following up with the interviewer.

My advice to the readers is not to bother/spam the interviewers with constant messages and conversations, because these will make them dislike you and want to avoid you. When they form aversion towards you, they will even less likely consider you for the job. Therefore, minimize follow ups to three times, and with good reasons to do so.

The first follow up is as soon as one day after the interview. Do not meet the interviewer in person, but send a "thank you" card, hand delivered to the receptionist, attention to the interviewer.

This gesture while trivial, will jog the memory of the interviewer about you, and bring an understated but potent "good will" effect in place, where in the subconscious, the interviewer may be nudged slightly to "return" this gratitude. But do note that it's important to just send "thank you" cards, and nothing of greater value, because the latter may count as attempts towards bribery, which will get everyone into trouble if investigated upon.

The second follow up should be timed to that date or period which had been agreed upon by the interviewers to update you, as well as during indefinite delays. When the interviewers didn't get back to you on time, it's rightful and reasonable for you as a concerned candidate to drop an email message to them to enquire about the status.

Do not make this a closed-ended question, but try to maneuver the question in a way, which will make them hesitate to reject you. You can suggest things within this email, like a special slide deck to offer more insights (I've talked about the inefficiency of offering too much before and during the first interview, but if you use this tactic as a strategic follow-up to increase chances of the next few interviews, it's not counted as a sunk cost fallacy).

The third follow up is made to establish network and remediation if any. This is deployed for two occasions- positive outcome: when you are slated for hire or subsequent interview rounds, and negative outcome: when your application is more or less formally turned down. What you'll need to do is to simply drop a message to the interviewer to request for connection on LinkedIn (if you haven't done so), and to keep in touch for future opportunities and communications.

If negative outcome seems imminent, the candidate should not let up any chances to seek recourse, especially after having gotten this far into the job search. In this third follow up, do open up an opportunity to resell yourself. We'll talk about this in greater details next.

Handling Delays and Objections

There are two outcomes that are undesirable after interviews, namely delays and objections. Delays are disheartening, because the lack of response and the uncertainty created by indefinite timeline increases the doubt of the job applicants towards the opportunity, particularly post-interviews. Whereas objections confirm that the candidate is not selected for the job after all, which is pretty much the unfortunate end of the job search.

Delays should not be held too negatively though, because there can be many open-ended reasons why it happened. The most common causes of delays are usually due to indecisiveness in the closure of a position normally caused by further reviews of the candidates, problems with the hiring processes which can be attributed to head count freeze, delay of budget, and other internal problems, and lastly, the sheer procrastination and/or negligence and complacency on the hirers' part. Every candidate should always be mindful of the fact that long delays in responses does not always mean that the company has dropped you; the process has simply lengthened.

However, do also bear in mind that delays can also happen due to negative reasons as well, when the candidate is no longer considered. That is as good as an objection, but then nobody will truly know, unless the hirers explicitly stated so.

If you're concerned, you can do several things. One way to check on the status of the opportunity is to look for any job postings made for the same opportunity after your interview; when the same job is advertised again, it could mean two things: the company was not satisfied with the last round of candidates and therefore tries to get more applications, or the opportunity is simply a phantom job, a device meant for collecting resumes and data. The second way to check, is to write directly to the stakeholders, the decision makers and the prospective supervisors in charge of filling this role, to see if the position has already been taken. The third way is to look at LinkedIn and see if this role has been filled up by a person.

I had mentioned previously that the second follow up can be applied when there are indefinite delays. Do write them to request for updates, to proactively suggest additional information (and value), and see if it can secure you a chance to get you to the next stage.

On the other hand, if the candidate is notified about not getting selected for this role, it counts towards a direct objection, which thus spells the end of the job application, almost.

However, before the candidate resign to fate, it's possible to take plausible routes of actions, rather than to give it up altogether. Here are some ways to handle objections.

1. **Offer to help**- When the interviewer delayed in responding to the candidate, it could be over procedural reasons or that the candidate had already been rejected. But since the candidates never truly know, it is always prudent to follow up and be helpful. When the delays seem unusually long and you don't get any responses, do write a note to the interviewer during the second follow up, stating that you're willing to step in to help out, to further clarify, submit additional documents and even request to give presentations. When I previously talked about the Pareto principle, I mentioned that there's no point in going the extra miles and effort on 20% of preferred company, yet if you've gotten far enough past first interview, more efforts invested may help you to positively influence the eventual outcome.

2. **Remediation**- When you are outrightly rejected, or when you discover that the same job you applied to have been put up again, you can choose to sound out to the hirer (avoid the interviewer this time if he or she is not the stakeholder, but go directly to the stakeholder) and request to know the reasons why you are not hired. If they do not respond, forget it, they are simply unprofessional and therefore such people are not worth working with. If they do, review the reasons and see if there are possible ways to remediate them, then do spell out to the stakeholder and sincerely ask to review you again. Express the willingness to renegotiate the terms for the job if you are desperate enough.

3. **Extension to other opportunities**- After you've been told you did not get the job, you'd still want to do a third follow up to connect with the hirer anyway, because this opportunity closed may lead you to other opportunities opened. Do ask the hirer if there are other opportunities available within the company or if it's possible to get you referred to other contacts who might be able to help you out. If there aren't any, at least ask them to KIV your profile for future use. Do not expect them to help you any further, because most likely they won't.

4. **Extreme Measures**- When you find out that you are not selected, and yet the position has not officially closed, you might want to attempt to go all out, depending on how much you really want this job. I will go through several strategies (which involve certain risks) next, for those who care enough to try out the last resorts to salvage this opportunity.

Deus ex Machina

Warning! This section is not for the faint of heart. But if the opportunity meant everything to you and you are passed up, it may be worth your while to throw caution to the wind to see if things can turn around, by employing the last resort, the device to hijack the machine to work in your favor. This move is a bit of a gamble, though not as terrifying as it sounds. What you'll do may fail or backfire, but rest assure that they are not dangerous enough to bring greater damage to yourself than displeasure from the hirer and discomfort on your part.

When the offer is given to the other person, it's usually too late to do anything, as the hirers would not want to break the agreement and inconvenience themselves and the chosen candidate. However, there's usually a window between rejection of applicants, and putting out offer.

What I'd like you to focus and work on is to attempt to influence their decisions in the window period. When you receive the confirmation of rejection, this window happens immediately after. If the hirers are delaying on you, with no notifications in that indefinite period, you should consider to take actions as soon as possible.

Granted that hirers, especially from reputable companies tend not to compromise, there's a high chance that they will shake off your last-ditch effort to influence their decisions. To compromise is to show that they have forfeited their power and authority, and admission of their mistakes in not hiring you. But your attempt is not primarily aimed at influencing the hirers. Your attempt can be escalated upwards to higher stakeholders when the hirers are not supportive.

Before we reveal some of the moves for your consideration, let's assess the critical points that surround any attempts in re-negotiation. Firstly, there must be no signs of emotional blackmailing or threats given at any point in this attempt. These things will not make them endear to the candidates, and will likely turn very ugly if they decide to take legal actions.

Secondly, everything is to be done within legal limits. You would not want to stir and bring any trouble to yourself over such a thing like getting a job opportunity. If the job opportunity warrants such trouble, it's wiser to look at other alternatives.

Thirdly, forget about any request to compare with other candidates. No matter how much you ask, the companies reserve the right not to share with you who is the preferred candidate, or who is applying to the job, because they have to abide with privacy laws.

Your re-negotiation should involve some kind of value proposition to the company, to appeal to their practical needs. You'd like to show them that by getting you onboard, it's going to be the best decision they make for the role. Here are the steps you can consider:

1. **Competition proposition**- This is a first level approach. Upon getting the rejection notification, or when the delay seems ridiculous, you may want to

state either of two things: a) that you are going to be hired by a competitor of the company soon, and you'd like them to seriously consider you because you like them better, or b) you have valuable competitor-related info that you'd not want them to miss out on, and that you'll gladly help them once you get hired. At this first level, you can propose such terms to the interviewer, but if he or she is not receptive. Consider other steps.

2. **Escalation to other authority**- For all you know, the interviewer may not like you, but it doesn't mean that other stakeholders wouldn't. This is a bit of a desperate and slightly dangerous effort, and it may involve a significant amount of risk if the interviewer becomes your boss when you get the job, because you've influenced his or her boss to get you hired. You may face a politically charged future thereafter but that really depends on how much you want the job. But if the interviewers are mere conduits, like HR managers, then by all mean appeal to the true stakeholders. When the interviewer ignores you, write to the likely stakeholders and appeal to them with your value propositions to make them consider you.

3. **The Test-Outs**- You can do either of two things to the interviewers or stakeholders: a) get them to test you out for a temporary role (with maybe lower pay) concurrently with the chosen person and if you've proven to be better, get you hired instead. Well, this is a contentious proposal, and will likely disadvantage you for a while, but you still get to be in the company anyway right? Only do this when you are certain that

the company has already decided to hire someone else. b) ask them to consider you after few months if the chosen candidate is not to their satisfaction. Tell them that you'll wait for them, because you are very keen and feel yourself most suited to this role.

Remember, these moves are slightly risky and may fail or backfire, but they can also bring great successes in turning a supposedly hopeless job application around. That ultimately depends on your risk appetite and how much you want that job. But of course, it will probably be much easier to look out for and apply to other opportunities if this endeavor is not worth the effort in your opinion.

A Promise is Nothing Without a Contract

Congratulations if you've finally clinched an offer! But do not let your guard down at this critical juncture. Talk is cheap, unless it's finalized on paper. I've heard of many instances whereby the supposed job offers are retracted and rescinded at the last minute, by companies citing all kinds of excuses like head-count freezes or choice of another preferred candidates. However, once the contract is inked, it's usually hard for the companies to go back on their words.

What you'd like to do is to make sure the contract can be finalized as soon as possible after they gave you their words. The first thing you'd like to do is to save the paper trail of the confirmation. Try to get everything in black and white about their promises. If they verbalize to you about their intent, try to request for an email confirmation. These can serve as evidence shall they choose to change their mind later.

The next thing you'd like to do is to ensure that they are able to give you a date or timeline for the finalization of the contract. Do make sure that the contract comes sooner than the actual start date so you can go through this contract and negotiate where necessary. When they give you a late date for the final signing, try to see if this can be brought forward by requesting to review the terms first. If they refuse, you can only count on them to keep to their words.

Afterword

If you still did not get the job despite everything that had been done, do not feel discouraged. If you've not had success for a while, do not lose hope and keep trying. There's a time and place for everything, and sometimes the many closed doors can lead to better opportunity. I had personally faced joblessness before about a decade ago (in 2009) during the global economic recession.

Looking back retrospectively, I was glad that I did not get the opportunities which rejected me, because I subsequently landed a job of my dream. One of that lost opportunity turned out to be a blessing in disguise, because that company subsequently folded and I had ex-employees of that company telling me about the horrifying ordeals they faced during their period of employment there. Incidentally that missed opportunity was the one which I wanted badly and felt sorely disappointed when it did not materialize during those periods of unemployment.

I thought about it and got quite philosophical later. It felt as if I was blessed and guided by the invisible hands of God away from harm and a bad outcome. Of course, I felt rather differently during those periods of unemployment because I was desperate, miserable and almost lost all hope and self-esteem, starting to doubt my own capability and lack of luck. It then turned out otherwise.

When you don't get a certain job, scoff at that one and look at the other. You are simply not meant to get that job, because a better one is destined for you. If you don't hear back from anyone, take it as a greater plan to get you away from those jobs, towards a better plan for you.

I've known of people who did exceedingly well after they decided to leave the employment market and started out on their own, accomplishing far greater heights than they would have ever imagined. And of course, if entrepreneurship is not your thing, there are also many people (like the account I quoted), who managed to get to a better place after a seemingly hopeless spell and dearth of luck and opportunities.

After reading this book, do count yourself as better prepared than the rest. In these trying times, your insights, resourcefulness and ingenuity will be put to the test, and you'll likely emerge better than the rest. You will be pre-disposed towards greater success when you cease to think like everybody else, as you get away from the masses in the middle, forging your own path towards the outliers where unimagined successes are found.

Other Books By the Author

A Cynical Guide to Power, Self Esteem & Social Bullying

Feeling powerless and oppressed? Peer into the secret laws of power not mentioned before in other books and engineer your endeavor to get back power, grow in power and improve your self-esteem.

A Cynical Guide to Corporate Jobs & Office Politics

Suffering from work politics and lack of career advancement? Learn contrarian and ingenious ways to maneuver favorable outcome towards your career development, while employ strategies and tactics to deal with politicking colleagues.

ABOUT THE AUTHOR

Rick Lazarus had previously written several critically acclaimed books under a different name. This book is the second in the series of instructive guides offering novel, and contrarian insights and secret strategies to enable the readers to survive and thrive in any situations. His life mission is to empower the disenfranchised. He enjoys doing all of the above in privacy and reclusion.

Website: https://ricklazarus.com

www.ingramcontent.com/pod-product-compliance
Lightning Source LLC
Chambersburg PA
CBHW071508140726
47997CB00005B/1900